Cities in a World Economy
Second Edition

Saskia Sassen
University of Chicago

PINE FORGE PRESS
Thousand Oaks   London   New Delhi

For information:

Pine Forge Press
A Sage Publications Company
2455 Teller Road
Thousand Oaks, California 91320
E-mail: sales@pfp.sagepub.com

Sage Publications Ltd.
6 Bonhill Street
London EC2A 4PU
United Kingdom

Sage Publications India Pvt. Ltd.
M-32 Market
Greater Kailash I
New Delhi 110 048 India

Publisher: Stephen D. Rutter
Assistant to the Publisher: Ann Makarias
Editorial Assistant: Cindy Bear
Copy Editor: Linda Gray
Typesetter: Marion Warren

Printed in the United States of America

03 10 9 8 7 6 5 4 3 2

Library of Congress Cataloging-in-Publication Data

Sassen, Saskia.
    Cities in a world economy / by Saskia Sassen.— 2nd ed.
        p. cm. — (Sociology for a new century)
    Includes bibliographical references and index.
    ISBN 0-7619-8696-0 (cloth: alk. paper).
    ISBN 0-7619-8666-9 (pbk.: alk. paper)
    1. Urban economics. 2. Metropolitan areas—Cross-cultural studies.
    3. Cities and towns—Cross-cultural studies. 4. Sociology, Urban. I.
    Title. II. Series.
    HT321 .S28 2000
    330.91732'2—dc21   99-050706

World Economy
Second Edition

ONE WEEK LOAN

Sociology for a New Century

A PINE FORGE PRESS SERIES

Edited by Charles Ragin, Wendy Griswold, and Larry Griffin

Sociology for a New Century brings the best current scholarship to today's students in a series of short texts authored by leaders of a new generation of social scientists. Each book addresses its subject from a comparative, historical, and global perspective and, in doing so, connects social science to the wider concerns of students seeking to make sense of our dramatically changing world.

- *An Invitation to Environmental Sociology*   Michael M. Bell

- *Global Inequalities*   York W. Bradshaw and Michael Wallace

- *Schools and Societies*   Steven Brint

- *Economy/Society*   Bruce Carruthers and Sarah Babb

- *How Societies Change*   Daniel Chirot

- *Ethnicity and Race: Making Identities in a Changing World*
  Stephen Cornell and Douglas Hartmann

- *The Sociology of Childhood*   William A. Corsaro

- *Cultures and Societies in a Changing World*   Wendy Griswold

- *Crime and Disrepute*   John Hagan

- *Gods in the Global Village: The World's Religions in Sociological Perspective*   Lester R. Kurtz

- *Waves of Democracy: Social Movements and Political Change*   John Markoff

- *Development and Social Change: A Global Perspective,* 2nd Edition
  Philip McMichael

- *Aging, Social Inequality, and Public Policy*   Fred C. Pampel

- *Constructing Social Research*   Charles C. Ragin

- *Women and Men at Work*   Barbara Reskin and Irene Padavic

- *Cities in a World Economy,* 2nd Edition   Saskia Sassen

- *Gender, Family, and Social Movements*   Suzanne Staggenborg

Contents

List of Exhibits

ABOUT THE AUTHOR

Saskia Sassen is Professor of Sociology at the University of Chicago and Centennial Visiting Professor at the London School of Economics. Her recent books are *Guests and Aliens* (1999), *Globalization and Its Discontents* (1998), and *Losing Control? Sovereignty in an Age of Globalization.* (1996). Her books have been translated into 10 languages. Her project "Cities and Their Crossborder Networks," sponsored by the United Nations, will be published by the United Nations University Press in 2000, and she is completing her research project "Governance and Accountability in a Global Economy." She is the main editor of the volume on urban sustainability in the new 14-volume encyclopedia on sustainability being produced by UNESCO.

ABOUT THE PUBLISHER

Pine Forge Press is a new educational publisher, dedicated to publishing innovative books and software throughout the social sciences. On this and any other of our publications, we welcome your comments, ideas, and suggestions. Please call or write to:

Pine Forge Press
A Sage Publications Company
31 St. James Ave., Suite 510
Boston, MA 92116
(617) 753-7512
E-mail: sdr@pfp.sagepub.com)

Visit our World Wide Web site, your direct link to a multitude of online resources: www.pineforge.com

Foreword

Sociology for a New Century offers the best of current sociological thinking to today's students. The goal of the series is to prepare students, and—in the long run—the informed public, for a world that has changed dramatically in the last three decades and one that continues to astonish.

This goal reflects important changes that have taken place in sociology. The discipline has become broader in orientation, with an ever growing interest in research that is comparative, historical, or transnational in orientation. Sociologists are less focused on "American" society as the pinnacle of human achievement and more aware of global processes and trends. They also have become less insulated from surrounding social forces. In the 1970s and 1980s, sociologists were so obsessed with constructing a science of society that they saw impenetrability as a sign of success. Today, there is a greater effort to connect sociology to the ongoing concerns and experiences of the informed public.

Each book in this series offers in some way a comparative, historical, transnational, or global perspective to help broaden students' vision. Students need to comprehend the diversity in today's world and to understand the sources of diversity. This knowledge can challenge the limitations of conventional ways of thinking about social life. At the same time, students need to understand that issues that may seem specifically "American" (for example, the women's movement, an aging population bringing a strained social security and health care system, racial conflict, national chauvinism, and so on) are shared by many other countries. Awareness of commonalities undercuts the tendency to view social issues and questions in narrowly American terms and encourages students to seek out the experiences of others for the lessons they offer. Finally, students need to grasp phenomena that transcend national boundaries—trends and processes that are supranational (for example, environmental degradation). Recognition of global processes stimulates student awareness of causal forces that transcend national boundaries, economies, and politics.

Saskia Sassen's new edition of *Cities in a World Economy* does this in two ways. First, it shows how certain characteristics of our turn-of-the-millennium flows of money, information, and people have led to the emergence of a new social formation: global cities. Whereas many urban theorists had previously suggested that cities were rendered economically obsolete by global telecommunications and the mobility of people and capital, *Cities in a World Economy* reveals how developments in the past decade suggest otherwise. This book, now updated to include the latest data available, introduces students to the way some cities—including New York, Tokyo, London, São Paulo, Hong Kong, and Sydney among others—have evolved from regional centers of culture and commerce to transnational market "spaces." These developments give new meaning to such fixtures of urban sociology as the centrality of place and the importance of geography in our social world. Second, this book examines the impact of global processes on the social structure of cities, showing how transformations in the organization of labor, the redistribution of earnings, and the restructuring of consumption are contributing to new hierarchies of inequality, both within and among cities around the world. Sassen convincingly makes the case that we need a "new geography," and indeed a new sociology, to comprehend the cities of the 21st century.

Preface to the Second Edition

Since I completed this book in the early 1990s, the world has seen a recession come to an end, a boom in global financial transactions, and a major crisis in Southeast Asia, parts of Latin America, and Russia. Yet throughout these often sharp and massive shifts, we have also seen the continuation of the major developments that I used to specify the features of the global economy that have made cities strategic. Indeed, many of the updated tables in this edition show the accentuation of some of the trends identified in the earlier edition. They also show the growth of the cross-border network of cities that constitutes a transnational space for the management and servicing of the global economy. As countries adopt the new rules of the global game, their major business centers become the gateways through which capital and other resources enter and exit their economies.

A major new trend that is becoming evident over the last few years is the strengthening of the networks connecting cities, including a novel development: the formation of strategic alliances between cities through their financial markets. The growth of global markets for finance and specialized services, the need for transnational servicing networks due to sharp increases in international investment, the reduced role of the government in the regulation of international economic activity, and the corresponding ascendance of other institutional arenas, notably global markets and corporate headquarters—all these point to the existence of a series of transnational networks of cities. We can see here the formation, at least incipient, of transnational urban systems. To a large extent, it seems to me that the major business centers in the world today draw their importance from these transnational networks. The global city is a function of a network—and in this sense, there is a sharp contrast with the erstwhile capitals of empires. This subject is sufficiently new and so little known that I have added a whole new section on this subject in Chapter 5.

These networks of major international business centers constitute new geographies of centrality. The most powerful of these new geographies of centrality at the global level bind the major international financial and business centers: New York, London, Tokyo, Paris, Frankfurt, Zurich, Amsterdam, Los Angeles, Sydney, and Hong Kong, among others. But this geography now also includes cities such as Bangkok, Seoul, Taipei, São Paulo, Mexico City, and Buenos Aires. The intensity of transactions among these cities, particularly through the financial markets, trade in services, and investment, has increased sharply, and so have the orders of magnitude involved. At the same time, there has been a sharpening inequality in the concentration of strategic resources and activities between each of these cities and others in the same country.

One of the more controversial sections of the first edition of this book proved to be my analysis and conceptualization of the growth of inequality within these cities. Then and now, the data are inadequate to have definitive proof. Yet I would argue that we continue to see this trend toward inequality. There is an ongoing growth of the highly paid professional classes connected to leading sectors of the global economy and of national economies. And there is also continuing growth of low-wage service workers, including industrial services. In many of these cities, we continue to see a fairly large middle class. But on closer examination, a good part of this middle class is still living at the level of prosperity it gained in the earlier economic phase. It is not certain at all that the sons and daughters of these aging middle classes in various cities around the world will have the, albeit modest, prosperity enjoyed by their parents. Furthermore, the growth of disadvantaged sectors, many excluded from a growing range of institutional worlds—of work, education, and politics—continues to be evident in many of these cities.

It has been fascinating to revisit the earlier empirical information and bring it up to date. The strengthening of many of these patterns took even me a bit by surprise.

Acknowledgments

Returning to a book written many years ago to update it is not easy. It is a little like entering a house long closed up. One's mind and imagination have moved on to other inquiries. If there is one single person who made this new edition possible, it is Kathleen Fernicola. Without her work and engagement with the subject, this updating might have languished. She did an astounding amount of work in a rather short period of time. I want to thank Harel Shapira for his intelligent research assistance and for making the whole process more enjoyable for all of us involved, and Jeremy

Bendik-Keymer, for his help with this edition. Thanks also go to the following reviewers for their helpful comments about this edition: Emily A. Copeland, Florida International University; Laura Hecht, California State University, Bakersfield; Christopher Mele, State University of New York at Buffalo; David R. Meyer, Brown University; Adam Weinberg, Colgate University; and Clifford J. Wirth, University of New Hampshire. Finally, I want to thank Steve Rutter, the publisher of Pine Forge Press, for giving me this opportunity, and Linda Gray for her excellent copyediting.

Preface to the First Edition

Sociologists have tended to study cities by looking at the ecology of urban forms and the distribution of population and institutional centers or by focusing on people and social groups, lifestyles, and urban problems. These approaches are no longer sufficient. Economic globalization, accompanied by the emergence of a global culture, has profoundly altered the social, economic, and political reality of nation-states, cross-national regions, and—the subject of this book—cities. Through the study of the city as one particular site in which global processes take place, I seek to define new concepts useful to understand the intersection of the global and the local in today's world—and tomorrow's.

It is helpful in this context to recall Janet Abu-Lughod, a leading urban sociologist, who has commented that it is impossible to study the city only from a sociological perspective because it requires an understanding of many other realities. Manuel Castells, another major urban sociologist, has added that it is impossible to study the city only from an urban perspective. These two observations mark an empty space in urban sociology, which I seek to address in this book.

Although there has been an international economic system for many decades and a world economy for many centuries, the current situation is distinct in two respects. On the one hand, we have seen the formation of transnational spaces for economic activity where governments play a minimal role, different from the role they once had in international trade for instance. Examples of such spaces are export processing zones, offshore banking centers, and many of the new global financial markets. On the other hand, these transnational spaces for economic activity are largely located in national territories under the rule of sovereign states. There is no such entity as a global economy completely "out there," in some space that exists outside nation-states. Even electronic markets and firms operating out of the World Wide Web have some aspect of their operation partly embedded in actual national territories. Yet the location of the global largely in the national happens through a significant new development: a change in the ways in which the national state regulates and governs at least part of its economy. Deregulation and privatization are but partial descriptions of this change. The outcome is the formation of transnational spaces inside the national. This new configuration is increasingly being called a global economy to distinguish it from earlier formations such as the old colonial empires or the international economic system of the immediate post-World War II period, in which governments played a crucial regulatory role in international trade, investment, and financial markets.

Understanding how global processes locate in national territories requires new concepts and research strategies. The global city is one such new concept; it draws on and demands research practices that negotiate the intersection of macroanalysis and ethnography. It presumes that global processes, from the formation of global financial markets to the rapid growth of transnational labor markets, can be studied through the particular forms in which they materialize in places.

This book shows how some cities—New York, Tokyo, London, São Paulo, Hong Kong, Toronto, Miami, and Sydney, among others—have evolved into transnational "spaces." As such cities have prospered, they have come to have more in common with one another than with regional centers in their own nation-states, many of which have declined in importance. Such developments require all those interested in the fate of cities to rethink traditionally held views of cities as subunits of their nation-states or to reassess the importance of national geography in our social world. Moreover, the impact of global processes radically transforms the social structure of cities themselves—altering the organization of labor, the distribution of earnings, the structure of consumption, all of which in turn create new patterns of urban social inequality. In *Cities in a World Economy*, I seek to provide the vocabulary and analytic frames with which students and the general reader can grasp this new world of urban forms.

Acknowledgments

I want to thank several individuals and institutions that made it possible to write this book in a rather brief period of time. The Wissenschaftszentrum in Berlin was a generous and intellectually stimulating home. So was the Institute for Advanced Studies in Vienna, most particularly because of Rainer Baubock and the students in my course. These institutions made all the difference in my 1991-1992 sabbatical year in Europe. The Russell Sage Foundation, where I was a visiting scholar in 1992-1993, is well known for its dedicated support of scholars and their work; I want to thank its staff and, most particularly, Vivian Kauffman for her precise and intelligent assistance. The Department of Political Science and the Faculty of Environmental Studies of York University in Toronto sponsored an international summer institute on the global city that allowed me to work with students from a variety of countries and backgrounds; I am particularly thankful to Roger Keil and Leo Panic. Finally, an invitation from the Woodrow Wilson International Center for Scholars to spend the summer of 1993 in Washington, D.C., provided me with the support to complete this book; I am especially grateful to Blair Ruble, Joseph Tulchin, and the members of the Urban Working Group: Paulo Singer, Richard Sennett, and Wilbur Zelinsky. I want to thank the excellent research assistance of Laura Bosco and Mark Williamson at the Woodrow Wilson Center; and Brian Sahd, Kam Wong, and Luc Nadal at Columbia University. Finally, Larry Griffin, Wendy Griswold, and Charles Ragin—the editors of the series—came up with the timely idea of the series; I am glad they convinced me to join the project.

The largest single debt is to Steve Rutter, founding editor of Pine Forge Press; Chiara Huddleston, associate publisher; Victoria Nelson, editor; and Anne Draus of Scratchgravel Publishing Services. Their help, patience, and—it must be said—relentlessness made this book possible, swimming as it was in a sea of other deadlines.

As always, Richard Sennett and Hilary Koob-Sassen were there.

1

Place and Production
in the Global Economy

At the end of the 20th century, massive developments in telecommunications and the ascendance of information industries led analysts and politicians to proclaim the end of cities. Cities, they told us, would become obsolete as economic entities. With large-scale relocations of offices and factories to less congested and lower-cost areas than central cities, computerized workplaces can be located anywhere: in a clerical "factory" in the Bahamas or in a home in the suburbs. The growth of information industries means that more and more outputs can be transmitted around the globe instantaneously. And the globalization of economic activity suggests that place—particularly the type of place represented by cities—no longer matters.

But this is a partial account. These trends are indeed all taking place, yet they represent only half of what is happening. Alongside the well-documented spatial dispersal of economic activities, we are seeing the growth of new forms of territorial centralization in top-level management and control operations. National and global markets, as well as globally integrated operations, require central places where the work of running global systems gets done. Furthermore, information industries require a vast physical infrastructure containing strategic nodes with a hyperconcentration of facilities. Finally, even the most advanced information industries have a production process that is partly place-bound.

Once these processes are brought into the analysis, funny things happen; secretaries become part of it, and so do the cleaners of the buildings where professionals work. An economic configuration very different from that suggested by the concept of **information economy** emerges. We recover the material conditions, production sites, and place-boundedness that are also part of globalization and the information economy. A detailed examination of the activities, firms, markets, and physical infrastructure involved in globalization, and concentrated in cities, allows us to see the actual role played by cities in a global economy. Thus, when tele-communications were introduced on a large scale in all advanced industries in the 1980s, we saw the central business districts of the leading cities and international business centers of the world—New York, Los Angeles, London, Tokyo, Paris, Frankfurt, São Paulo, Hong Kong, and Sydney, among others—reach their highest density of firms ever. This explosion in the numbers of firms located in the downtown areas of major cities in the 1980s and 1990s goes against what should have been expected according to models emphasizing territorial dispersal; this is especially true when one considers the high cost of locating in a major downtown area.

If telecommunications have not made cities obsolete, have they at least altered the economic function of cities in a global economy? And if this is so, what does it tell us about the importance of place and locale in an era dominated by the imagery and language of economic globalization and information flows? Is there a new and strategic role for major cities, a role linked to the formation of a truly global economic system, a role not sufficiently recognized by analysts and policymakers? And could it be that the reason this new and strategic role has not been sufficiently recognized is that economic globalization—what it actually takes to implement global markets and processes—is misunderstood?

The notion of a global economy has become deeply entrenched in political and media circles all around the world. Yet its dominant images— the instantaneous transmission of money around the globe, the information economy, the neutralization of distance through **telematics**— are partial, and hence profoundly inadequate, representations of what globalization and the rise of information economies actually entail for the concrete life of cities. Missing from this abstract model are the actual material processes, activities, and infrastructures crucial to the implementation of globalization. Overlooking the spatial dimension of economic globalization and overemphasizing the information dimensions both have served to distort the role played by major cities in the current phase of economic globalization.

The last 20 years have seen pronounced changes in the geography, composition, and institutional framework of economic globalization. Although a world economy has been in existence for several centuries, it has been repeatedly reconstituted over time. A key starting point for this book is the fact that in each historical period, the world economy has consisted of a distinct configuration of geographic areas, industries, and institutional arrangements. One of the most important changes over the last 20 years has been the increase in mobility of capital at both the national and especially the transnational levels. This transnational mobility of capital has brought about specific forms of articulation among different geographic areas and transformations in the role played by these areas in the world economy. This trend in turn has produced several types of locations for international transactions, the most familiar of which are **export processing zones** and **offshore banking centers**. One question for us, then, is the extent to which major cities are yet another type of *location* for international transactions in our world economy, although clearly one at a very high level of complexity.

Increased capital mobility not only brings about changes in the geographic organization of manufacturing production and in the network of financial markets, but it also generates a demand for types of production needed to ensure the management, control, and servicing of this new organization of manufacturing and finance. These new types of production range from the development of telecommunications to specialized services that are key inputs for the management of a global network of factories, offices, and financial markets. The mobility of capital also includes the production of a broad array of innovations in these sectors. These types of production have their own locational patterns; they tend toward high levels of agglomeration. We will want to ask whether a focus on the *production* of these service inputs illuminates the question of place in processes of economic globalization, particularly the kind of place represented by cities.

Specialized services for firms and financial transactions, as well as the complex markets connected to these regions of the economy, are a layer of activity that has been central to the organization of major global processes beginning in the 1980s. To what extent is it useful to think in terms of the broader category of cities as key locations for such activities—in addition to the more narrowly defined locations represented by headquarters of transnational corporations or offshore banking centers—to further our understanding of major aspects of the world economy's organization and management?

Much of the scholarly literature on cities has focused on internal aspects of the urban social, economic, and political systems, and it has considered cities to be part of national urban systems. International aspects typically have been considered the preserve of nation-states, not of cities. The literature on international economic activities, moreover, has traditionally focused on the activities of multinational corporations and banks and has seen the key to globalization in the *power* of multinational firms. Again, this conceptualization has had the effect of leaving no room for a possible role for cities.

Including cities in the analysis adds three important dimensions to the study of economic internationalization. First, it breaks down the nation-state into a variety of components that may be significant in understanding international economic activity. Second, it displaces our focus from the power of large corporations over governments and economies to the range of activities and organizational arrangements necessary for the implementation and maintenance of a global network of factories, service operations, and markets; these are all processes only partly encompassed by the activities of transnational corporations and banks. Third, it contributes to a focus on place and on the urban social and political order associated with these activities of the global network. Processes of economic globalization are thereby reconstituted as concrete production complexes situated in specific places containing a multiplicity of activities and interests, many unconnected to global processes. Focusing on cities allows us to specify a geography of strategic places on a global scale, as well as the microgeographies and politics unfolding within these places.

A central thesis organizing this book is that the last two decades have seen transformations in the composition of the world economy, accompanied by the shift to services and finance, that have renewed the importance of major cities as sites for certain types of activities and functions. In the current phase of the world economy, it is precisely the combination of the global dispersal of economic activities *and* global integration—under conditions of continued concentration of economic ownership and control—that has contributed to a strategic role for certain major cities. These I call **global cities** (Sassen 1991). Some have been centers for world trade and banking for centuries. Yet beyond these long-standing functions, today's global cities are (1) command points in the organization of the world economy; (2) key locations and marketplaces for the leading industries of the current period—finance and specialized services for firms; and (3) major sites of production for these industries, including the production of innovations in these industries. Several cities also fulfill equivalent functions on the smaller geographic scales of both trans- and subnational regions. Furthermore, whether at the global or at the regional level, these cities must inevitably engage each other in fulfilling their functions, as the new forms of growth seen in these cities are a result of these networks of cities. There is no such entity as a single global city.

Alongside these new global and regional hierarchies of cities is a vast territory that has become increasingly peripheral, increasingly excluded from the major processes that fuel economic growth in the new global economy. Many formerly important manufacturing centers and port cities have lost functions and are in decline, not only in the less developed countries but also in the most advanced economies. This is yet another meaning of economic globalization. We can think of these developments as constituting new geographies of centrality that cut across the old divide of poor/rich countries, and of new geographies of marginality that also cut across the poor/rich country divide.

The most powerful of these new geographies of centrality binds together the major international financial and business centers: New York, London, Tokyo, Paris, Frankfurt, Zurich, Amsterdam, Sydney, and Hong Kong, among others. But this geography now also includes cities such as São Paulo, Mexico City, Bombay, Buenos Aires, and Seoul. The intensity of transactions among these cities, particularly through financial markets, flows of services, and investment has increased sharply, and so have the orders of magnitude involved. At the same time, there has been a sharpening inequality in the concentration of strategic resources and activities between each of these cities and others in their respective countries. For instance, Paris now concentrates a larger share of leading economic sectors and wealth in France than it did 20 years ago, whereas Marseilles, once a major economic center, has lost its own share and is suffering severe decline. Some national capitals, for example, have lost central economic functions and power to the new global cities, which have taken over some of the coordination functions, markets, and production processes once concentrated in national capitals or in major regional centers. A case in point, São Paulo has gained immense strength as a business and financial center in Brazil over Rio de Janeiro—once the capital and most important city in the country—and over the once powerful axis represented by Rio and Brasilia, the current capital. This is one of the meanings, or consequences, of the formation of a globally integrated economic system.

What is the impact of this type of economic growth on the broader social and economic order of these cities? A vast literature on the impact of a dynamic, high-growth manufacturing sector in highly developed countries shows that it raises wages, reduces economic inequality, and contributes to the formation of a middle class. There is much less literature about the impact on the service economy, especially the rapidly growing specialized services.

Specialized services, which have become a key component of all developed economies, are not usually analyzed in terms of a production or work process. Such services are usually seen as a type of output—that is, high-level technical expertise. Thus, insufficient attention has been paid to the actual array of jobs, from high paying to low paying, involved in the production of these services. A focus on production displaces the emphasis from expertise to work. Services need to be produced, and the buildings that hold the workers need to be built and cleaned. The rapid growth of the financial industry and of highly specialized services generates not only high-level technical and administrative jobs but also low-wage unskilled jobs. Together with the new interurban inequalities mentioned above, we are also seeing new economic inequalities within cities, especially within global cities and their regional counterparts.

The new urban economy is in many ways highly problematic. This is perhaps particularly evident in global cities and their regional counterparts. The new growth sectors of specialized services and finance contain capabilities for profit making vastly superior to those of more traditional economic sectors. The latter are essential to the operation of the urban economy and the daily needs of residents, but their survival is threatened in a situation in which finance and specialized services can earn superprofits. This sharp polarization in the profit-making capabilities of different sectors of the economy has always existed. But what we see happening today takes place on a higher order of magnitude, and it is engendering massive distortions in the operations of various markets, from housing to labor. We can see this effect, for example, in the unusually sharp increase in the beginning salaries of MBAs and lawyers in the corporate sector and in the fall, or stagnation, in the wages of low-skilled manual workers and clerical workers. We can see the same effect in the retreat of many real estate developers from the low- and medium-income housing market who are attracted to the rapidly expanding housing demand by the new highly paid professionals and the possibility for vast overpricing of this housing supply.

The rapid development of an international property market has made this disparity even worse. It means that real estate prices at the center of New York City are more connected to prices in London or Frankfurt than to the overall real estate market in the city. In the 1980s, powerful institutional investors from Japan, for instance, found it profitable to buy and sell property in Manhattan or central London. In the 1990s, this story has multiplied many times. German, Dutch, French, and U.S. investors are buying properties in central London and in major cities around the world. They force prices up because of the competition and raise them even further to sell at a profit. How can a small commercial operation in these cities compete with such investors and the prices they can command?

The high profit-making capability of the new growth sectors rests partly on speculative activity. The extent of this dependence on speculation can be seen in the crisis of the early 1990s that followed the unusually high profits in finance and real estate in the 1980s. That real estate and financial crisis, however, seems to have left the basic dynamic of the sector untouched, and we saw prices and stock market values reach new highs by the mid-1990s—only to have yet another crisis in 1997-98 and, once again, enormous increases as the decade closes. These crises can thus be seen as a temporary adjustment to more reasonable (i.e., less speculative) profit levels. The overall dynamic of polarization in profit levels in the urban economy remains in place, as do the distortions in many markets.

The typical informed view of the global economy, cities, and the new growth sectors does not incorporate these multiple dimensions. Elsewhere, I have argued that we could think of the dominant narrative or mainstream account of economic globalization as a narrative of eviction (Sassen 1996). In the dominant account, the key concepts of globalization, information economy, and telematics all suggest that place no longer matters and that the only type of worker that matters is the highly educated professional. This account favors (1) the capability for global transmission over the concentrations of material infrastructure that make transmission possible; (2) information outputs over the workers producing those outputs, from specialists to secretaries; and (3) the new transnational corporate culture over the multiplicity of cultural environments, including reterritorialized "immigrant" cultures within which many of the "other" jobs of the global information economy take place. In brief, the dominant narrative concerns itself with the upper circuits of capital, not the lower ones.

This narrow focus has the effect of excluding from the account the *place*-boundedness of significant components of the global information economy; it thereby also excludes a whole array of activities and types of workers from the story of globalization that are in their own way as vital to it as international finance and global telecommunications are. Failing to include these activities and workers ignores the variety of cultural contexts within which they exist, a diversity as present in processes of globalization as is the new international corporate culture. When we focus on place and production, we can see that globalization is a process involving not only the corporate economy and the new transnational corporate culture but also, for example, the immigrant economies and work cultures evident in our large cities.

The new empirical trends and the new theoretical developments are making cities prominent once again for a still small but growing number of social scientists and cultural theorists. Cities have reemerged not only as objects of study but also as strategic sites for the theorization of a broad array of social, economic, and political processes central to the current era: (1) economic globalization and international migration, (2) the emergence of specialized services and finance as the leading growth sector in advanced economies, (3) new types of inequality, (4) the new politics of identity and culture, (5) the dynamics of radicalization, and (6) the politics of space. In this context, it is worth noting that we are also seeing the beginning of a repositioning of cities in policy arenas. Two instances in particular stand out. One is the recent programmatic effort at the World Bank to produce analyses that show how important urban economic productivity is to macroeconomic performance. The other is the explicit competition among major cities to gain direct access, bypassing national states, to increasingly global markets for resources and activities ranging from foreign investment, headquarters, and international institutions to tourism and conventions. The mayors of a growing number of cities worldwide have set up offices for foreign economic affairs and appear increasingly interested in dealing directly with mayors of other countries.

The subject of the city in a world economy is extremely broad. The literature on cities is inevitably vast, but it focuses mostly on single cities. It is also a literature that is mostly domestic in orientation. International studies of cities tend to be comparative. What is lacking is a transnational perspective on the subject: that is to say, one that takes as its starting point a dynamic system or set of transactions that by its nature entails multiple locations involving more than one country. This contrasts with a comparative international approach, which focuses on two or more cities that may have no connections between each other.

Given the vastness of the subject and of the literature on cities and given what is lacking in much of that literature, this book focuses particularly on recent empirical and conceptual developments because they are an expression of major changes in urban and national economies and in modes of inquiry about cities. Such a choice is inevitably limited and certainly cannot account for the cases of many cities that may *not* have experienced any of these developments. Our focus on the urban impact of economic globalization, the new inequalities among and within cities, and the new urban economy is justified by the major characteristics of the current historical period and the need for social scientists to address these changes.

Chapter 2 examines key characteristics of the global economy that are important for an understanding of the impact of globalization on cities. Chapter 3 analyzes the new interurban inequalities, focusing on three key issues: (1) the impact of globalization, particularly the internationalization of production and the growth of tourism, on so-called **primate urban systems** in less developed countries; (2) the impact of economic globalization on so-called **balanced urban systems;** and (3) the possibility of the formation of a transnational urban system. A rapidly growing research literature now finds sharp increases in the linkages binding the cities that function as production sites and marketplaces for global capital. Chapter 4 focuses on the new urban economy, where finance and specialized services have emerged as driving engines for profit making. Chapter 5 examines these issues in greater detail through a series of case studies of key global cities and related issues. Chapter 6 focuses on possible new urban forms and social alignments inside these cities to understand whether these are merely a quantitative transformation or also a qualitative one. Chapter 7 considers this and other possibilities in summarizing the central propositions of this book.

2

The Urban Impact of Economic Globalization

Profound changes in the composition, geography, and institutional framework of the global economy have had major implications for cities. In the 1800s, when the world economy consisted largely of trade, the crucial sites were harbors, plantations, factories, and mines. Cities were already servicing centers at that time: The major cities of the time typically developed alongside harbors, and trading companies depended on multiple industrial, banking, and other commercial services located in cities. Cities, however, were not the key production sites for the leading industries in the 1800s; the production of wealth was centered elsewhere. Today, international trade continues to be an important fact in the global economy, but it has been overshadowed both in value and in power by international financial flows, whether loans and equities or foreign currency transactions. In the 1980s, finance and specialized services emerged as the major components of international transactions. The crucial sites for these transactions are financial markets, advanced corporate service firms, banks, and the headquarters of transnational corporations (TNCs). These sites lie at the heart of the process for the creation of wealth, and they are located in cities.

Thus, one of the factors influencing the role of cities in the new global economy is the change in the composition of international transactions, a factor often not recognized in standard analyses of the world economy. The current composition of international transactions shows this transformation very clearly. For instance, foreign direct investment (FDI) grew three times faster in the 1980s than the growth of the export trade. Furthermore, by the mid-1980s, investment in services had become the main component in FDI flows, whereas before it had been in manufacturing or raw materials extraction. These trends became even sharper in the 1990s. By 1999, the monetary value of international financial flows was vastly larger than the value of international trade and FDI. The sharp growth of international financial flows has raised the level of complexity of transactions. This new circumstance demands a highly advanced infrastructure of specialized services and top-level concentrations of telecommunications facilities. Cities are central locations for both.

The first half of this chapter will present a somewhat detailed account of the geography, composition, and institutional framework of the global economy today. The second half will focus on two types of strategic places for international financial and service transactions: global cities and offshore banking centers. Finally, we will consider the impact of the collapse of the Pax Americana on the world economy and the subsequent shift in the geographical axis of international transactions.

The Global Economy Today

Here we emphasize new investment patterns and dominant features of the current period. The purpose is not to present an exhaustive account of all that constitutes the world economy today. It is rather to discuss what distinguishes the current period from the immediate past.

Geography

A key feature of the global economy today is the geography of the new types of international transactions. When international flows consist of raw materials, agricultural products, or mining goods, the geography of transactions is in part determined by the location of natural resources. Historically, this has meant that a large number of countries in Africa, Latin America, and the Caribbean were key sites in this geography. When finance and specialized services became the dominant component of international transactions in the early 1980s, the role of cities was strengthened. At the same time, the sharp concentration in these industries means that now only a limited number of cities play a strategic role.

The fact of a new geography of international transactions becomes evident in FDI flows—that is, investors acquiring a firm, wholly or in part, or building and setting up new firms in a foreign country (see UNCTAD 1993). FDI flows are highly differentiated in their destination and can be constituted through many different processes. During the last two decades, the growth in FDI has been embedded in the internationalization of production of goods and services. The internationalization of production in manufacturing is particularly important in establishing FDI flows into developing countries.

Compared with the 1950s, the 1980s saw a narrowing of the geography of the global economy and a far stronger East-West axis. This is evident in the sharp growth of investment and trade within what is often referred to as the *triad:* the United States, Western Europe, and Japan. FDI flows to developed countries grew at an average annual rate of 24% from 1986 to 1990, reaching a value of US$129.6 billion in 1991, out of a total worldwide FDI inflow of US$159.3 billion (see Exhibit 2.1). By the mid-1980s, 75% of all FDI stock and 84% of FDI stock in services was in developed countries. There was a sharp concentration even among developed countries in these patterns: The top four recipient countries (United States, United Kingdom, France, and Germany) accounted for half of world inflows in the 1980s; the five major exporters of capital (United States, United Kingdom, Japan, France, and Germany) accounted for 70% of total outflows. In the early 1990s, there were declines in most of these figures due to the financial crisis, but by the late 1990s, levels of investment had grown sharply, reaching US$233.1 billion in developed countries and US$148.9 in developing countries. Overall, worldwide FDI inflows went from US$175.8 billion in 1992 to US$400.5 billion in 1997 (see Exhibit 2.1). Financial concentration is evident in a ranking of the top banks in the world, with only eight countries represented (see Exhibit 2.2 and also Chapter 5).

Although investment flows in developing countries in the 1990s were lower than in developed countries, they were high in historic terms—a fact that reflects the growing internationalization of economic activity (see Exhibit 2.1). International investment in developing countries lost share in the 1980s, although it increased in absolute value and regained share by the early 1990s. Since 1985, FDI has been growing at an annual rate of 22%, compared with 3% from 1980 to 1984, and 13% from 1975 to 1979. Yet the share of worldwide flows going to developing countries as a whole fell from 26% to 17% between the early 1980s and the late 1980s, pointing to the strength of flows within the triad (United States, Western Europe, and Japan); it grew in the 1990s, reaching 37.2% by 1997 before the financial crisis of the late 1990s. Most of the flow to developing countries has gone into East, South, and Southeast Asia, where the annual rate of growth rose on the average by over 37% a year in the 1980s and 1990s.

There was a time when Latin America was the single largest recipient region of FDI. Between 1985 and 1989, Latin America's share of total flows to developing countries fell from 49% to 38%, and Southeast Asia's share rose from 37% to 48%. However, the absolute increase in FDI has been so sharp that, notwithstanding a falling share, Latin America has actually experienced increases in the amount of FDI, especially toward the end of the 1980s and in the 1990s (although these increases are mostly concentrated

EXHIBIT 2.1

Inflows and Outflows of Foreign Direct Investment (FDI), 1986 to 1997 (in US$ billions and percentages)

Year	Developed Countries		Developing Countries		Central and Eastern Europe		All Countries	
	Inflows	Outflows	Inflows	Outflows	Inflows	Outflows	Inflows	Outflows
Value (US$ billions)								
1986-1991	129.6	169.2	29.1	11.3	0.7	0.0	159.3	180.5
1992	120.3	180.0	51.1	20.7	4.4	1.0	175.8	200.8
1993	138.9	205.8	72.5	34.9	6.1	0.2	217.6	240.9
1994	141.5	241.5	95.6	42.5	5.9	0.3	243.0	284.3
1995	211.5	306.5	105.5	45.6	14.2	0.4	331.2	352.5
1996	195.4	283.5	129.8	49.2	12.3	0.9	337.6	333.6
1997	233.1	359.2	148.9	61.1	18.4	3.3	400.5	423.7
Share in total (percentage)								
1986-1991	81.3	93.7	12.3	0.1	0.0*	0.00*	100.0	100.0
1992	68.4	89.6	29.1	10.3	2.5	0.0	100.0	100.0
1993	63.8	85.4	33.3	14.5	2.8	0.0	100.0	100.0
1994	58.2	85.0	39.3	15.0	2.4	0.0	100.0	100.0
1995	63.9	86.9	31.9	12.9	4.3	0.0	100.0	100.0
1996	57.9	85.0	38.5	14.7	3.7	0.0	100.0	100.0
1997	58.2	84.4	37.2	14.4	4.6	0.1	100.0	100.0
Growth rate (percentage)								
1992	-7	6	76	83	575	308	10	11
1993	15	14	42	69	38	58	24	20
1994	2	17	32	22	-4	66 ⁻	12	18
1995	49	27	10	7	140	52	36	24
1996	-8	-8	23	8	-13	143	2	-5
1997	19	27	15	24	49	232	19	27

Note: Asterisk (*) denotes that the share in total FDI inflows and outflows was below 0.01 and 0.001, respectively.

Source: Based on UNCTAD *World Investment Report* (1998:361-71).

EXHIBIT 2.2

Top Banks in the World Ranked by Assets, 1998 (US$ millions)

Asset Rank	Name	City	Assets	Net Income
1	Bank of Tokyo (22)—Mitsubishi (6)	Tokyo	752,318	352
2	Deutsche Bank (11)	Frankfurt	575,693	1,441
3	Sumitomo Bank (2)	Osaka	513,781	294
4	Dai-Ichi Kangyo Bank (1)	Tokyo	476,696	-1,531
5	Fuji Bank (4)	Tokyo	474,371	942
6	Sanwa Bank (5)	Tokyo	470,336	223
7	ABN Amro Holdings (16)	Amsterdam	444,410	1,790
8	Sakura Bank (3)	Tokyo	470,336	153
9	Industrial & Commercial Bank	Beijing	435,723	622
10	HSBC Holdings	London	405,037	5,330
11	Norinchukin Bank (9)	Tokyo	400,031	267
12	Industrial Bank of Japan (10)	Tokyo	399,509	110
13	Dresdner Bank (24)	Frankfurt	389,626	999
14	Banque Nationale de Paris (12)	Paris	358,187	743
15	Société Générale (20)	Paris	342,760	876
16	Chase Manhattan	New York	336,099	2,461
17	Union Bank of Switzerland (26)	Zurich	325,082	-261
18	Commerzbank	Frankfurt	320,419	773
19	Barclays Bank (13)	London	318,551	2,807
20	National Westminister Bank (18)	London	317,411	752
21	Crédit Lyonnais (9)	Paris	312,926	39
22	Mitsubishi Trust & Banking (15)	Tokyo	312,223	97
23	Westdeutsche Landesbank	Duesseldorf	305,879	441
24	Tokai Bank (14)	Nagoya	296,895	145
25	Cle. Financiè de Paribas	Paris	293,437	838
26	Bank of China	Beijing	292,554	1,067
27	Citicorp (29)	New York	277,653	3,788
28	Swiss Bank	Geneva	268,161	-1,461
29	Sumitomo Trust & Banking (17)	Osaka	266,035	63
30	Bayerische Vereinsbank	Munich	256,371	527

Note: Numbers in parentheses denote standing in 1991. Five banks have dropped out of the top 50 from 1991: Mitsui Trust and Banking Co. Ltd. (19), Kyowa Saltama Bank Ltd. (23), Daiwa Bank (25), Yasuda Trust and Banking Co. Ltd. (27), Instituto Bancario San Paulo di Torino (28). Three banks are still in the top 50 but not reported in the table above: Long-Term Credit Bank (previous rank, 21/35), Crédit Agricole (8/35), and Toyo Trust and Banking (30/48).

Source: Based on *Hoover's Handbook of World Business* (1998).

in a few countries). These figures point to the emergence of Southeast Asia as a crucial transnational space for production. The Asian region has surpassed Latin America and the Caribbean for the first time ever as the largest host region for FDI in developing countries.

The other two major components of the global economy are trade and financial flows other than FDI. By its very nature, the geography of trade is less concentrated than that of direct foreign investment. Wherever there are buyers, sellers are likely to go. Finance, on the other hand, is enormously concentrated; it is described later in the book.

Composition

In the 1950s, the major international flow was world trade, concentrated in raw materials, other primary products, and resource-based manufacturing. In the 1980s, the gap between the growth rate of exports and that of financial flows widened sharply. Although there are severe problems with measurement, the increase in financial and service transactions, especially the former, is so sharp as to leave little doubt (see Exhibit 2.3). For instance, worldwide outflows of FDI nearly tripled between 1984 and 1987, grew another 20% in 1988, and grew yet another 20% in 1989. By 1990, total worldwide stock of FDI stood at US$1.5 trillion and at US$2 trillion by 1992. After the 1981-82 slump and up to 1990, global FDI grew at an average of 29% a year, a historic high. Furthermore, the shares of the tertiary sector grew consistently over the 1980s and 1990s while that of the primary sector fell. Between 1992 and 1997, worldwide FDI inflows grew by 56%. FDI worldwide outward stock stood at US$3.5 trillion in 1997.

Many factors have fed the growth of FDI: (1) Several developed countries became major capital exporters, most notably Japan; (2) the number of cross-border mergers and acquisitions grew sharply; and (3) the flow of services and transnational service corporations have emerged as major components in the world economy. Services, which accounted for about 24% of worldwide stock in FDI in the early 1970s, had grown to 50% of stock and 60% of annual flows by the end of the 1980s. The single largest recipient of FDI in services in the 1980s—the decade of high growth of these flows—was the European Community, yet another indication of a very distinct geography in world transactions. But it should be noted that these flows have also increased in absolute terms in the case of less developed countries.

Another major transformation has been the sharp growth in the numbers and economic weight of TNCs—firms that operate in more than one country through affiliates, subsidiaries, or other arrangements. The central role played by TNCs can be seen in the fact that U.S. and foreign TNCs accounted for 80% of international trade in the United States in the late

EXHIBIT 2.3

Sectoral Distribution of FDI Stock for the Largest Developed Home Countries and the Largest Developed and Developing Host Countries, Selected Years, 1970 to 1990 (US$ billion and percentages)

Group of Countries and Sectors	Billions of Dollars					Average Annual Growth Rate in Percentages					Share in Percentages				
	1970	1975	1980	1985	1990	1971-1975	1976-1980	1981-1985	1986-1990	1981-1990	1970	1975	1980	1985	1990
A. Outward stock															
Developed countries[a]															
Primary	29	58	88	115	160	14	8.7	5.5	6.8	6.2	22.7	25.3	18.5	18.5	11.2
Secondary	58	103	208	240	556	11.7	15.1	2.9	18.3	10.3	45.2	45	43.8	38.7	38.7
Tertiary	41	68	179	265	720	10.4	21.4	8.2	22.1	14.9	31.4	27.7	37.7	42.8	50.1
Total	129	229	475	620	1436	11.7	15.7	5.5	18.3	11.7	100	100	100	100	100
B. Inward stock															
Developed countries[b]															
Primary	12	17	18	39	94	4.7	5.9	16.7	19.2	18	16.2	12.1	6.7	9.2	9.1
Secondary	44	79	148	195	439	10.7	13.4	5.7	17.6	11.5	60.2	56.5	55.2	46.2	42.5
Tertiary	17	44	102	188	499	16.5	18.3	13	21.6	17.2	23.7	31.4	38.1	44.5	48.4
Total	73	140	268	422	1032	11.3	13.9	9.5	19.6	14.4	100	100	100	100	100
Developing countries/economies[c]															
Primary	—	7	17	31	46	—	19.4	12.8	8.2	10.5	—	20.6	22.7	24	21.9
Secondary	—	19	41	64	102	—	16.6	9.3	9.8	9.5	—	55.9	54.6	49.6	48.6
Tertiary	—	8	17	34	62	—	16.3	14.9	12.8	13.8	—	23.5	22.7	26.4	29.5
Total	—	34	75	129	210	—	17.1	11.4	10.2	10.8	100	100	100	100	100

a. Australia, Canada, France, Federal Republic of Germany, Italy, Japan, Netherlands, United Kingdom, and United States; together, these countries accounted for almost 90% of outward FDI stock in 1990. 1970 and 1971 to 1975 growth data exclude Australia and France.

b. Australia, Canada, France, Federal Republic of Germany, Italy, Japan, Netherlands, United Kingdom, Spain, and United States; together, these countries accounted for approximately 72% of total inward FDI stock in 1990. 1970 and 1971 to 1975 growth data exclude Australia, France, and Spain.

c. Argentina, Brazil, Chile, China, Colombia, Hong Kong, Indonesia, Malaysia, Mexico, Nigeria, Philippines, Republic of Korea, Singapore, Taiwan Province of China, Thailand, and Venezuela; together, these countries accounted for 68% of total inward FDI in developing countries.

Source: UNCTD, Programme on Transnational Corporations, *World Investment Report* (1993:62).

1980s (UNCTC 1991:chap. 3). By 1997, global sales generated by foreign affiliates of TNCs were valued at US$9.5 trillion, while worldwide exports of goods and services were at US$7.4 trillion, of which one-third was intra firm trade (UNCTD 1998). More than 143 countries have adopted special FDI regimes to attract FDI, up from 20 in 1982 (UNCTD 1998: chap. 3).

Institutional Framework

How does the "world economy" cohere as a system? We cannot take the world economy for granted and assume that it exists simply because international transactions do. One question raised by the developments described above is whether the global economic activities occurring today represent a mere quantitative change or actually entail a change in the international regime governing the world economy. Elsewhere, I have argued that the ascendance of international finance and services produces a new regime with distinct consequences for other industries, especially manufacturing, and for regional development, insofar as regions tend to be dominated by particular industries (Sassen 1991). One consequence of this new regime is that TNCs have become even more central to the organization of the world economy, and the new, or vastly expanded older, global markets are now an important element in the institutional framework.

In addition to financing huge government deficits, the financial credit markets that exploded into growth in the 1980s served the needs of TNCs to a disproportionate extent. TNCs also emerged as a source for financial flows to developing countries, both through direct inflows of FDI and indirectly, insofar as FDI stimulates other forms of financial flows. In some respects, TNCs replaced banks. [1] The bank crisis of 1982 sharply cut bank loans to developing countries to the point that the aggregate net flow of financial resources to developing countries was negative during much of the 1980s. For better or for worse, the TNC is now a strategic organizer of what we call the world economy.

Global financial markets have emerged as yet another crucial institution organizing the world economy. The central role of markets in international finance, a key component of the world economy today, was in part brought about by the so-called Third World bank crisis formally declared

---

1. FDI by transnationals may be financed through transnational banks or through the international credit markets. The mid-1980s saw a sharp increase in the share of the latter and a sharp decline in the former (see Sassen 1991:chap. 4).

in 1982. This was a crisis for the major transnational banks in the United States, which had made massive loans to Third World countries and firms incapable of repayment. The crisis created a space into which small, highly competitive financial firms moved, launching a whole new era in the 1980s in speculation, innovation, and levels of profitability. The result was a highly unstable period but one with almost inconceivably high levels of profits that fed a massive expansion in the volume of international financial transactions. Deregulation was another key mechanism facilitating this type of growth, centered in internationalization and in speculation. Markets provided an institutional framework that organized these massive financial flows. Notwithstanding two financial crises, one in 1990-91 and the second in 1997-98, the end of the 1990s saw a sharp growth in the value of financial transactions.

The formation of transnational trading blocs is yet another development that contributes to the new institutional framework. The two major blocs are the North American Free Trade Agreement (NAFTA) and the European Economic Community (EEC). According to the World Trade Organization (WTO), there were over 70 regional trade agreements by the late 1990s. The specifics of each of the two major trading blocs currently being implemented vary considerably, but both strongly feature the enhanced capability for capital to move across borders. Crucial to the design of these blocs is the free movement of financial services. Trade, although it has received far more attention, is less significant; there already is a lot of trade among the countries in each bloc, and tariffs are already low for many goods. The NAFTA and EEC blocs represent a further formalization of capital as a transnational category, one that operates on another level from that represented by TNCs and global financial markets. Finally, in 1993, the WTO was set up to oversee cross-border trade. It has the power to adjudicate in cross-border disputes between countries and represents potentially a key institutional framework for the governance of the global economy.

Considerable effort and resources have gone into the development of a framework for governing global finance. This includes the development of new institutional accounting and financial reporting standards, minimum capital requirements for banks, and efforts to institute greater transparency in corporate governance.

These realignments have had pronounced consequences. One consequence of the extremely high level of profitability in the financial industry, for example, was the devaluing of manufacturing as a sector—although not necessarily in all subbranches. Much of the policy around deregulation had the effect of making finance so profitable that it took investment away from manufacturing. Finance also contains the possibility for superprofits by maximizing the circulation of and speculation in money—that is, buying and selling—in a way that manufacturing does not (e.g., securitization, multiple transactions over a short period of time, selling debts). Securitization, which played a crucial role, refers to the transformation of various types of financial assets and debts into marketable instruments. The 1980s saw the invention of numerous ways to securitize debts, a trend that has continued in the 1990s with the invention of ever more complex and speculative instruments. A simple illustration is the bundling of a large number of mortgages that can be sold many times, even though the number of houses involved stays the same. This option is basically not available in manufacturing. The good is made and sold; once it enters the realm of circulation, it enters another set of industries, or sector of the economy, and the profits from subsequent sales accrue to these sectors.

These changes in the geography and in the composition of international transactions, and the framework through which these transactions are implemented, have contributed to the formation of new strategic sites in the world economy. This is the subject of the next section.

Strategic Places

Three types of places above all others symbolize the new forms of economic globalization: export processing zones, offshore banking centers, high-tech districts, and global cities. There are also many other locations where international transactions materialize. Certainly, harbors continue to be strategic in a world of growing international trade and in the formation of regional blocs for trade and investment. And massive industrial districts in major manufacturing export countries, such as the United States, Japan, and Germany, are in many ways strategic sites for international activity and specifically for production for export. None of these locations, however, captures the prototypical image of today's global economy the way the first four do. Some geographers now speak of global city regions to capture this development.

Because much has been published about export processing zones and high-tech districts, and because they entail types of activity less likely to be located in cities than finance and services, we will not examine them in detail. As they are less known, let me define the first as zones in low-wage countries where firms from developed countries can locate factories to process and/or assemble components brought in from and reexported to the developed countries. Special legislation was passed in several developed countries to make this possible. The central rationale for these zones is access to cheap labor for the labor-intensive stages of a firm's production process. Tax breaks and lenient workplace standards in the zones are additional incentives. These zones are a key mechanism in the internationalization of production.

Here we will focus briefly on global cities and offshore banking centers.

Global Cities

Global cities are strategic sites for the management of the global economy and the production of the most advanced services and financial operations. They are key sites for the advanced services and telecommunications facilities necessary for the implementation and management of global economic operations. They also tend to concentrate the headquarters of firms, especially firms that operate globally. The growth of international investment and trade and the need to finance and service such activities have fed the growth of these functions in major cities. The erosion of the role of the government in the world economy, which was much larger when trade was the dominant form of international transaction, has displaced some of the organizing and servicing work from governments and major headquarters to specialized service firms and global markets in services and finance. Here we briefly examine these developments, first by presenting the concept of the global city and then by empirically describing the concentration of major international markets and firms in various cities.

The specific forms assumed by globalization over the last decade have created particular organizational requirements. The emergence of global markets for finance and specialized services, along with the growth of investment as a major type of international transaction, has contributed to the expansion in command functions and in the demand for specialized services for firms. Much of this activity is not encompassed by the organizational form of the TNC or bank, even though these types of firms account for a disproportionate share of international flows. Nor is much of this activity encompassed by the power of transnationals, a power often invoked to explain the fact of economic globalization. It involves work and workers. Here some of the hypotheses developed in our recent work are of interest, especially those that examine the spatial and organizational forms of economic globalization and the actual work of running transnational economic operations (Sassen 1991). This way of framing the inquiry has the effect of recovering the centrality of place and work in processes of economic globalization.

A central proposition in the global city model (Sassen 1991) is that the *combination* of geographic dispersal of economic activities and system integration that lies at the heart of the current economic era has contributed to a strategic role for major cities. Rather than becoming obsolete because of the dispersal made possible by information technologies, cities instead concentrate command functions. In a somewhat different vocabulary, Friedmann and Wolff (1982) posited this long before it exploded into the research literature it is now (see also Friedmann 1986; Sassen-Koob 1982).[2] To this role, I have added two additional functions: (1) Cities are postindustrial production sites for the leading industries of this period—finance and specialized services—and (2) cities are transnational marketplaces where firms and governments from all over the world can buy financial instruments and specialized services.

The territorial dispersal of economic activity at the national and world scale implied by globalization has created new forms of concentration. This territorial dispersal and ongoing concentration in ownership can be inferred from some of the figures on the growth of transnational enterprises and their affiliates. Exhibit 2.4 shows how vast the numbers of affiliates of TNCs are. This raises the complexity of management functions, accounting, and legal services, and hence the growth of these activities in global cities.

In the case of the financial industry, we see a similar dynamic of global integration: a growth in the number of cities integrated in the global financial network and a simultaneous increase of concentration of value managed at the top of the hierarchy of centers. We can identify two distinct phases. Up to the end of the 1982 Third World debt crisis, the large transnational banks dominated the financial markets in terms of both the volume and the nature of financial transactions. After 1982, this dominance was increasingly challenged by other financial institutions and the major innovations they produced. These challenges led to a transformation in the leading components of the financial industry, a proliferation of financial institutions, and the rapid internationalization of financial markets. The marketplace and the advantages of agglomeration—and hence, cities—assumed new significance beginning in the mid-1980s. These developments led simultaneously to (1) the incorporation of a multiplicity of

---

2. I have traced this emerging scholarly lineage in Sassen (2000). Some of the texts are Castells (1989); Fainstein (1993); Knox and Taylor (1995); Allen, Massey, and Pryke (1999); Short and Kim (1999); and Eade (1997).

EXHIBIT 2.4

Number of Parent Transnational Corporations and Foreign Affiliates, by Region and Country, Selected Years (1990-1997)

	Year	Parent Corporations Based in Country	Foreign Affiliates Located in Country
All Developed Countries	1990	33,500	81,800
	1996	43,442	96,620
Select countries			
Australia	1992	1,306	695
	1997	485	2,371
Canada	1991	1,308	5,874
	1996	1,695	4,541
Federal Republic of Germany	1990	6,984	11,821
	1996	7,569	11,445
France	1990	2,056	6,870
	1996	2,078	9,351
Japan	1992	3,529	3,150
	1996	4,231	3,014
Sweden	1991	3,529	2,400
	1997	4,148	5,551
Switzerland	1985	3,000	2,900
	1995	4,506	5,774
United Kingdom	1991	1,500	2,900
	1996	1,059	2,609
United States	1990	3,000	14,900
	1995	3,379	18,901
All Developing Countries	1990	2,700	71,300
	1996	9,323	230,696
Select countries			
Brazil	1992	566	7,110
	1995	797	6,322
China	1989	379	15,966
	1997	379	145,000
Colombia	1987	—	1,041
	1995	302	2,220
Hong Kong, China	1991	500	2,828
	1997	500	5,067
Indonesia	1988	—	1,064
	1995	313	3,472
Philippines	1987	—	1,952
	1995	—	14,802
Republic of Korea	1991	1,049	3,671
	1996	4,806	3,878
Singapore	1986	—	10,709
	1995	—	18,154
Central and Eastern Europe	1990	400	21,800
	1996	842	121,601
World Total	1990	36,600	174,900
	1996	53,607	448,917

Source: Based on UNCTAD, *World Investment Report* (1998:3, 4).

markets all over the world into a global system that fed the growth of the industry after the 1982 debt crisis and (2) new forms of concentration, specifically the centralization of the industry in a few leading financial centers. Hence, in the case of the financial industry, to focus only on the large transnational banks would exclude precisely those sectors of the industry where much of the new growth and production of innovations has occurred. Also, it would again leave out an examination of the wide range of activities, firms, and markets that compose the financial industry beginning in the 1980s.

The geographic dispersal of plants, offices, and service outlets and the integration of a growing number of stock markets around the world could have been accompanied by a corresponding decentralization in control and central functions. But this has not happened.

If we organize some of the evidence on financial flows according to the places where the markets and firms are located, we can see distinct patterns of concentration. The evidence on the locational patterns of banks and securities houses points to sharp concentration. For example, the worldwide distribution of the 100 largest banks and 25 largest securities houses in 1991 shows that Japan, the United States, and the United Kingdom accounted for 39 and 23 of each, respectively (see top half of Exhibits 2.5 and 2.6). This pattern persists in the late 1990s, notwithstanding multiple financial crises in the world and in Japan particularly (see bottom half of Exhibits 2.5 and 2.6).

The stock market illustrates this pattern well. From Bangkok to Buenos Aires, governments deregulated their stock markets to allow their participation in a global market system. And they have seen an enormous increase in the value of transactions. Yet there is immense concentration in leading stock markets in terms of worldwide capitalization—that is, the value of publicly listed firms. The market value of equities in domestic firms confirms the leading position of a few cities. In September 1987, before the stock market crisis, this value stood at US$2.8 trillion in the United States and at US$2.89 trillion in Japan. Third ranked was the United Kingdom, with US$728 billion. The extent to which these values represent extremely high levels is indicated by the fact that the next largest value was for West Germany, a major economy where capitalization stood at US$255 billion, a long distance from the top three. What these levels of stock market capitalization represent in the top countries is indicated by a comparison with gross national product (GNP) figures: in Japan, stock market capitalization was the equivalent of 64%; in the United States, the equivalent of 119%; in the United Kingdom, the equivalent of 118% of GNP; and in Germany, 23% of GNP. The full impact of deregula-

EXHIBIT 2.5

United States, Japan, and United Kingdom: Share of World's 50 Largest Banks, 1991 and 1997 (US$ millions and percentage)

	No. of Firms	Assets	% of Top 50	Capital	% of Top 50
			1991		
Japan	27	6,572,416	40.7	975,192	40.6
United States	7	913,009	5.7	104,726	4.4
United Kingdom	5	791,652	4.9	56,750	2.4
Subtotal	39	8,277,077	51.3	1,136,668	47.4
Total for Top 50	50	16,143,353	100.0	2,400,439	100.0

	No. of Firms	Assets	% of Top 50	Capital	% of Top 50
			1997		
Japan	12	6,116,307	36.4	1,033,421	45.8
United States	6	1,794,821	10.7	242,000	10.7
United Kingdom	5	1,505,686	9.0	130,587	5.8
Subtotal	23	9,416,814	56.0	1,406,008	62.3
Total for Top 50	50	16,817,690	100.0	2,257,946	100.0

Note: Ranked by assets as determined by Dow Jones Global Indexes in association with WorldScope; figures are based on each listed company's 1997 fiscal year results, except data on Japanese banks, which are based on fiscal 1998 results.

Source: Based on "World Business," *Wall Street Journal,* September 24, 1992, R27; "World Business," Wall Street Journal, September 28, 1998, R25-27.

tion and the growth of financial markets can be seen in the increases in value and in number of firms listed in all the major stock markets in the world by 1997 (see Table 2.7). The market value of listings rose between 1990 and 1997 from US$2.8 trillion to US$9.4 trillion in New York City and from US$1 trillion to US$2 trillion in London. Similar patterns, although at lower orders of magnitude, are evident in the other stock markets listed in Exhibit 2.7.

The concentration in the operational side of the financial industry is made evident in the fact that most of the stock market transactions in the leading countries are concentrated in a few stock markets. The Tokyo exchange accounts for 90% of equities trading in Japan. New York accounts for about two-thirds of equities trading in the United States; and London accounts for most trading in the United Kingdom. There is, then, a disproportionate concentration of worldwide capitalization in a few cities.

EXHIBIT 2.6

United States, Japan, and United Kingdom: Share of World's 25 Largest Security Firms, 1991 and 1997 (US$ millions and percentage)

			1991		
	No. of Firms	*Assets*	*% of Top 25*	*Capital*	*% of Top 25*
Japan	10	171,913	30.5	61,871	50.5
United States	11	340,558	60.4	52,430	42.8
United Kingdom	2	44,574	7.9	3,039	2.5
Subtotal	23	557,045	98.8	117,340	95.7
Total for Top 25	25	563,623	100.0	122,561	100.0
			1997		
	No. of Firms	*Assets*	*% of Top 25*	*Capital*	*% of Top 25*
Japan	6	236,712	11.9	36,827	14.1
United States	15	1,660,386	83.2	207,181	79.3
United Kingdom	2	41,396	2.1	9,501	3.6
Subtotal	23	1,938,494	97.1	253,509	97.1
Total for Top 25	25	1,995,782	100.0	261,180	100.0

Note: Ranked by capital as determined by Dow Jones Global Indexes; figures based on 1997 fiscal year results.
Source: Based on "World Business," *Wall Street Journal,* September 24, 1992, R27; "World Business," *Wall Street Journal,* September 28, 1998, R25-27.

Certain aspects of the territorial dispersal of economic activity may have led to some dispersal of profits and ownership. Large firms, for example, have increased their subcontracting to smaller firms worldwide, and many national firms in the newly industrializing countries have grown rapidly, thanks to investment by foreign firms and access to world markets, often through arrangements with transnational firms. Yet this form of growth is ultimately part of a chain in which a limited number of corporations continue to control the end product and reap most of the profits associated with selling on the world market. Even industrial homeworkers in remote rural areas are now part of that chain (Sassen 1988:chap. 4).

Under these conditions, the territorial dispersal of economic activity creates a need for expanded central control and management if this dispersal is to occur along with continued economic concentration. This in turn has contributed to the strategic role played by major cities in the world economy today.

EXHIBIT 2.7a

New York, Toyko, and London: Share of World Stock Market Value, 1990 and 1997 (US$ millions and number)

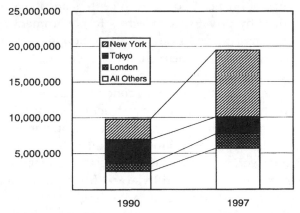

Source: Based on Meridian Securities Markets, *World Stock Exchange Fact Book* (1998).

Note: All others includes Frankfurt, Paris, Zurich, Toronto, Amsterdam, Milan, Sydney, Hong Kong, Singapore, Taiwan, and Seoul stock exchanges.

EXHIBIT 2.7b

Top Cities Ranked by Stock Market Value, 1990 and 1997 (US$ billions)

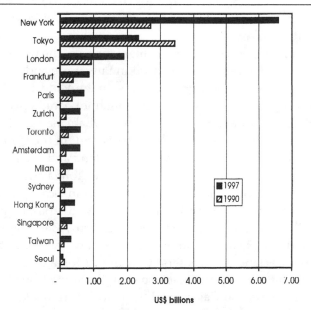

Source: Based on Meridian Securities Markets, *World Stock Exchange Fact Book* (1998).

Note: For Australia 1997, the number of listed companies is from 1996; when only domestic is listed, it represents the total market value.

Offshore Banking Centers

Offshore financial centers are another important spatial point in the worldwide circuits of financial flows. Such centers are above all else tax shelters, a response by private sector actors to government regulation. They began to be implemented in the 1970s, although international tax shelters have existed in various incipient forms for a long time. The 1970s marked a juncture between growing economic internationalization and continuing government control over the economy in developed countries, partly a legacy of the major postwar reconstruction efforts in Europe and Japan. Offshore banking centers are, to a large extent, paper operations. The Cayman Islands, for example, illustrate some of these issues (Roberts 1994). By 1997, they were ranked as the seventh largest international banking operation in the world and the fifth largest financial center after London, Tokyo, New York, and Hong Kong, according to International Monetary Fund (IMF) data (IMF 1999). They also were still the world's second largest insurance location with gross capital of US$8 billion in 1997. The value of deposits held in banks in the Cayman Islands grew from US$250 billion in 1990 to US$640 billion in 1997. Its 593 banks in 1997 included 47 of the world's top 50 banks. But even though that tiny country supposedly has well over 500 banks from all around the world, only 69 banks have offices there, and only 6 are "real" banks for cashing and depositing money and other transactions. Many of the others exist only as folders in a cabinet (Walter 1989; Roberts 1994).

These offshore centers are located in many parts of the world. The majority of Asian offshore centers are located in Singapore and Hong Kong; Manila and Taipei are also significant centers. In the Middle East, Bahrain took over from Beirut in 1975 as the main offshore banking center, with Dubai following as a close second. In 1999, Abu Dhabi made a bid to create its own offshore financial center on Saadiyat Island. In the South Pacific, we find major centers in Australia and New Zealand and smaller offshore clusters in Vanuatu, the Cook Islands, and Nauru; Tonga and Western Samoa are seeking to become such centers. In the Indian Ocean, centers cluster in the Seychelles and in Mauritius. In Europe, Switzerland tops the list, and Luxembourg is a major center; others are Cyprus, Madeira, Malta, the Isle of Man, and the Channel Islands. Several small places are struggling to compete with established centers: Gibraltar, Monaco, Liechtenstein, Andorra, and Campione. The Caribbean has Bermuda, the Cayman Islands, Bahamas, Turks and Caicos, and the British Virgin Islands.

Why do offshore banking centers exist? This question is especially pertinent given the massive deregulation of major financial markets in the

1980s and the establishment of "free international financial zones" in several major cities in highly developed countries. The best example of such free international zones for financial activity is the Euromarket, beginning in the 1960s and much expanded today, with London at the center of the Euromarket system. Other examples, as of 1981, were international banking facilities in the United States, mostly in New York City, that allowed U.S. banks to establish special adjunct facilities to accept deposits from foreign entities free of reserve requirements and interest rate limitations. Tokyo, finally, saw the development of a facility in 1986 that allowed transactions in the Asian dollar market to be carried out in that city; this meant that Tokyo got some of the capital being transacted in Hong Kong, Singapore, and Bahrain, all Asian dollar centers.

Compared with the major international centers, offshore banking centers offer certain types of additional flexibility: secrecy, openness to "hot" money and to certain "legitimate" options not quite allowed in the deregulated markets of major financial centers, and tax minimization strategies for international corporations. Thus, offshore centers are used not only for Euromarket transactions but also for various accounting operations aimed at tax avoidance or minimization.

In principle, the Euromarkets of London are part of the offshore markets. They were set up to avoid the system for regulating exchange rates and balance-of-payments imbalances contained in the Bretton Woods agreement of 1945. The Bretton Woods agreement set up a legal framework for the regulation of international transactions, such as foreign currency operations, for countries or banks wanting to operate internationally. Euromarkets were initially a Eurodollar market, where banks from the United States and other countries could do dollar transactions and avoid U.S. regulations. Over the last decade, other currencies have joined.

In finance, *offshore* does not always mean overseas or foreign; basically the term means that less regulation takes place than "onshore"—the latter describing firms and markets not covered by this special legislation (Roberts 1994). The onshore and offshore markets compete with each other. Deregulation in the 1980s brought a lot of offshore capital back into onshore markets, especially in New York and London—a not insignificant factor in convincing governments in these countries to proceed with deregulation of the financial markets in the 1980s. London's much-noted "Big Bang" and the less-noted "petit bang" in Paris are instances of such a process of deregulation of financial markets.

The Euromarkets are significant in international finance. According to the Bank for International Settlements, the Eurocurrency markets grew from US$9 billion in 1964 to US$57 billion in 1970 and US$661 billion in

1981. The oil crisis was important in feeding this growth. In the 1980s, it was Eurobonds and Eurosecurities—that is, bonds and securities traded "offshore," outside the standard regulatory framework. Securitization was crucial in the 1980s, to launch the new financial era by making liquid what had been illiquid forms of debt. With the launch of the euro in January 1999, Euromarkets are experiencing a period of profound change and growth, with the current value of outstanding international debt in both euro and legacy currencies at US$1,629 in 1998 (IMF 1999: Part 2).

Offshore banking centers basically grew out of tax havens in the 1970s, and this is one of the ways in which they differ from the Euromarkets. Some offshore centers today are mere tax havens, whereas some old tax havens have become full-fledged offshore banking centers; many offshore centers specialize in certain branches of banking, insurance, and other financial transactions. There is a clustering of small offshore banking centers within the time zone of each of the three major financial centers (New York City, London, Tokyo); these marginal offshore centers do some servicing of business being transacted in the major centers and within that time zone. But not all offshore activity is related to major centers, nor is location offshore totally determined by time zones.

In brief, offshore banking centers represent a highly specialized location for certain types of international financial transactions. They are also a buffer zone in case the governments of the leading financial centers in the world should decide to reregulate the financial markets. On the broader scale of operations, however, they represent a fraction of the financial capital markets now concentrated in global cities.

Conclusion: After the Pax Americana

The world economy has never been a planetary event; it has always had more or less clearly defined boundaries. Moreover, although most major industries were involved throughout, the cluster of industries that dominated any given period changed over time, contributing to distinct structurings of the world economy. Finally, the institutional framework through which the world economy coheres has also varied sharply, from the earlier empires through the quasi-empire of the Pax Americana—the period of U.S. political, economic, and military dominance—and its collapse in the 1970s.

It is in this collapse of the Pax Americana, when the rebuilt economies of Western Europe and Japan reentered the international markets, that we see emerging a new phase of the world economy. There is considerable agreement among specialists that in the mid-1970s new patterns in the world economy became evident. First, the geographical axis of international transactions changed from North-South to East-West. In this process, significant parts of Africa and Latin America became unhinged from their hitherto strong ties with world markets in commodities and raw materials. Second was a sharp increase in the weight of FDI in services and in the role played by international financial markets. Third was the breakdown of the Bretton Woods agreement, which had established the institutional framework under which the world economy had operated since the end of World War II. This breakdown was clearly linked to the decline of the United States as the single dominant economic power in the world. Japanese and European multinationals and banks became major competitors with U.S. firms. The financial crises in Asia in the 1990s have once again strengthened the role of the North-Atlantic system in the global economy.

These realignments are the background for understanding the position of different types of cities in the current organization of the world economy. A limited but growing number of major cities are the sites for the major financial markets and leading specialized services firms. And a large number of other major cities have lost their role as leading export centers for manufacturing, precisely because of the decentralization of production. This shift in roles among major cities in the new world economy will be the focus of the next chapter.

3

New Inequalities among Cities

The trends described in the preceding chapter point to the emergence of a new kind of urban system, one operating at the global and transnational regional levels. This is a system wherein cities are crucial nodes for the international coordination and servicing of firms, markets, and even whole economies that are increasingly transnational. These cities emerge as strategic places in the global economy. Most cities, however, including most large cities, are not part of these new transnational urban systems. Typically, urban systems are coterminous with nation-states.

Correspondingly, with rare exceptions (Chase-Dunn 1984; GaWC [Global Cities and World Cities Study Group and Network] 1998; Sassen 2000; Walters 1985), studies of city systems assume that the nation-state is the unit of analysis. We ask, What is the impact of economic globalization on national urban systems? Does the globalization of major industries, from auto manufacturing to finance, have distinct effects on different types of national urban systems? We will focus on the effects of the shift to services and economic globalization on balanced and primate urban systems, the two major types of urban systems that have been identified in the research literature on cities. Western European nations typically have been regarded as a good example of balanced urban systems; Latin American nations, as a good example of systems with high levels of primacy—that is, inordinate concentrations of population and major economic activities in one city, typically the national capital. The most recent research signals some sharp changes in these two regions.

In the first two sections of the chapter, we will examine the impact of economic globalization on these two types of urban systems. In the third section, we will turn to the emergence of **transnational urban systems.**

EXHIBIT 3.1

Select Cities in Latin America and the Caribbean, 1990

Impacts on Primate Systems: The Case of Latin America and the Caribbean

It is widely documented that many regions in the world—Latin America, the Caribbean, large parts of Asia, and to some extent Africa—have long been characterized by urban primacy (Abreu et al. 1989; Dogan & Kasarda 1988; Feldbauer et al. 1993; Hardoy 1975; Lee 1989; Linn 1983; Lozano & Duarte 1991; Stren & White, 1989). Primate cities account for a disproportionate share of population, employment, and gross national product (GNP), a fact illustrated by the figures presented in Exhibit 3.2. Thus, Greater São Paulo accounts for 36% of national domestic product (NDP)

Some indicators of the Estimated Economic Importance of Select Urban Areas Worldwide, various Years, 1970 to 1980 (in percentages)

Urban Area	Year	Population	Employment	Public Revenues	Public Expenditures	Output Measure
Brazil						
Greater São Paulo	1970	8.6	—	—	—	36.0 of NDP
						48.0 of net industrial product
China						
Shanghai	1980	1.2	—	—	—	12.5 of gross industrial product
Dominican Republic						
Santa Domingo	1981	24.0				70.0 of commercial and banking transactions
						56.0 of industrial growth
Ecuador						
Guayaquil[a]	1970	13.0	—	—	—	30.0 of GDP
Haiti						
All urban	1976	24.2	15.6			57.6 of national income
Port-au-Prince	—	15.0	7.7	47.2	82.7[b]	38.7 of national income
Other urban	—	9.2	7.9	—	—	18.9 of national income
India						
All urban	1970–71	19.9	17.7[c]			38.9 of NDP
Kenya						
All urban	1976	11.9	—	—	—	30.3 of income
Nairobi	—	5.2	—	—	—	20.0 of income
Other urban	—	6.7	—	—	—	10.3 of income
Mexico						
All urban	1970	60.0			(29.0)[d]	79.7 of personal income
Federal District	—	14.2				33.6 of personal income
Pakistan						
Karachi	1974–75	6.1				16.1 of GDP
Peru						
Lima	1980	28.0				43.0 of GDP
Philippines						
Metro Manila	1970	12.0	—	45.0		25.0 of GDP
Thailand						
Metro Bangkok	1972	10.9	14.0[e]		30.5[f]	37.4 of GDP
Turkey						
All urban	1981	47.0	42.0			70.0 of GNP
Tunisia						
Tunis	1975	16.0	17.2	—	—	

a. Guayas Province; b. Current expenditures only; c. Workers; d. Federal public investment only; e. 1970 data; f. 1969 data.

Source: Friedrich Kahnert, "Improving Urban Employment and Labor Productivity" (1987).

EXHIBIT 3.3

Population of 20 Largest Agglomerations, 1996 to 2015 (millions)

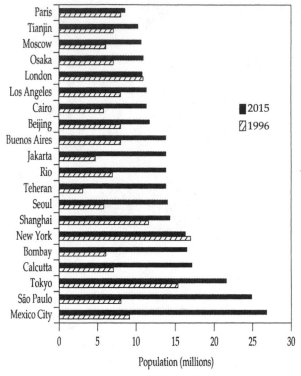

Population (millions)

Source: United Nations, *The Prospects of World Urbanization*, 1997.

and 48% of net industrial product in Brazil. Santo Domingo accounts for 70% of commercial and banking transactions and 56% of industrial growth in the Dominican Republic. And Lima accounts for 43% of gross domestic product (GDP) in Peru.

Primacy is not simply a matter of absolute size, nor is large size a marker of primacy. Several of the cities listed in Exhibit 3.2 are not necessarily among the largest in the world. Primacy is a relative condition that holds within a national urban system. Some of the largest urban agglomerations in the world do not necessarily entail primacy: New York, for example, is among the 20 largest in the world, but it is not a primate city given the multipolar nature of the urban system in the United States. Furthermore, primacy is not an exclusive trait of developing countries, even though its most extreme forms are to be found in the developing world: Tokyo and London are two cities that have elements of primacy. Finally, the emergence of so-called megacities may or may not be associated with primacy. The 20 largest urban agglomerations by 1996 and the foreseeable future include some cities that are not necessarily primate, such as New York, Los Angeles, Tianjin, Osaka, and Shanghai, and others that can be characterized as having low levels of primacy, such as Paris and Buenos Aires (see Exhibit 3.3).

Primacy and megacity status are clearly fed by urban population growth, a process that is expected to continue. The evidence worldwide points to the ongoing urbanization of the population, especially in developing countries. As in the developed countries, one component of urban growth in those countries is the suburbanization of growing sectors of the population. The figures in Exhibit 3.4 show rates of urban growth in select developing countries. The higher the level of development, the higher the urbanization rate is likely to be. Thus, a country like Argentina had an urbanization rate of 87.8% in 1994, which is quite similar to that of highly developed countries. In contrast, Algeria's urbanization rate of 55% and Nigeria's 38.5% in 1994 point to a rather different urbanization level from that in developed countries. Finally, there are countries such as India and China that have vast urban agglomerations, notwithstanding their very low rate of urbanization; they are, clearly, among the most populous countries in the world, and as a result, the information conveyed by an indicator such as the urbanization rate differs from that of the more typical case in terms of overall population size.

On the subject of primacy, the literature on Latin America shows considerable convergence in the identification of major patterns, along with multiple interpretations of these patterns. Many studies note that we are seeing sharper primacy rather than the emergence of the more balanced national urban systems we would expect with "modernization" (Edel 1986; El-Shakhs 1972; Roberts 1976; Smith 1985; Walters 1985). The disintegration of rural economies, including the displacement of small holders because of the expansion of large-scale commercial agriculture, and the continuing inequalities in the spatial distribution of institutional resources are recognized as key factors strengthening primacy (Kowarick, Campos, and de Mello 1991; Regional Employment Program for Latin America and the Caribbean [PREALC] 1987).

Less widely known and documented is the fact that in the 1980s a deceleration in primacy occurred in several, although not all, countries in Latin America. This trend will not eliminate the growth of megacities, but it is worth discussing in some detail because it represents in part an impact of economic globalization—concrete ways in which global processes implant themselves in particular localities. The overall shift in growth

EXHIBIT 3.4

Urban Growth Patterns in Select Developing Countries, Selected Periods, 1980 to 2025 (numbers and percentage)

Country	Per Capita GNP Level 1995 (US$)[a]	Size of Population (in 000s)[b]				Percentage of Urban Population[b]		Average Rate of Growth[b]			
		1994		2025				Urban Population (%)		Rural Population (%)	
		Urban	Rural	Urban	Rural	1994	2025	1980–1985	1990–1995	1980–1985	1990–1995
Argentina	8,030	30,006	4,176	43,083	3,050	87.8	93.4	1.9	1.6	-0.9	-1.3
Mexico	3,320	68,691	23,167	117,222	19,372	74.8	85.8	3.4	2.8	0.3	0.00
Colombia	1,910	24,939	9,606	41,532	7,827	72.2	84.1	3.1	2.4	0.3	-0.03
Brazil	3,640	123,450	35,694	204,791	25,459	77.6	88.9	3.7	2.7	-1.3	-1.4
Algeria	1,600	15,030	12,295	33,675	11,800	55.0	74.1	3.7	3.8	2.5	0.5
Morocco	1,110	12,684	13,804	26,917	13,733	47.9	66.2	4.3	3.1	1.4	1.2
Malaysia	3,890	10,422	9,273	22,942	8,635	52.9	72.7	4.5	3.9	1.1	0.9
Senegal	600	3,381	4,721	10,505	6,391	41.7	62.2	3.3	3.7	2.1	1.7
Côte d'Ivoire	660	5,915	7,865	23,611	13,206	42.9	64.1	6.6	5.0	2.5	2.6
Nigeria	260	41,722	66,745	146,948	91,449	38.5	61.6	6.1	5.2	2.2	1.7
Kenya	280	7,341	20,002	32,616	30,744	26.8	51.5	8.1	6.8	3.2	2.5
India	340	243,486	675,084	629,757	762,329	26.5	45.2	3.9	2.9	1.7	1.6
Indonesia	980	67,024	127,590	167,392	108,205	34.4	60.7	4.6	4.5	1.1	0.1
China	620	355,597	853,244	831,880	694,226	29.4	54.5	1.4	4.0	1.2	0.0

Sources: [a]The World Bank, *World Development Indicators* (1998); [b]U.N. Department for Economic and Social Information and Policy Analysis, *Urban and Rural Agglomerations* (1994).

strategies toward export-oriented development created growth poles that emerged as alternatives to the primate cities for migrants (Gilbert 1996; Landell-Mills, Agarwala, and Please 1989; Portes and Lungo 1992a, 1992b).[1] This shift was substantially promoted by the expansion of world markets for commodities and the foreign direct investment of multinational corporations.

One of the best sources of information on these developments is a large, collective, multicity study directed by Portes and Lungo (1992a, 1992b) that focused on the Caribbean region. [2] The Caribbean has a long history of urban primacy. Portes and Lungo studied the urban systems of Costa Rica, the Dominican Republic, Guatemala, Haiti, and Jamaica, countries that clearly reflect the immense variety of cultures and languages in this region. These countries represent a wide range of colonization patterns, ethnic compositions, economic development, and political stability. In the 1980s, export-oriented development, a cornerstone of the Caribbean Basin Initiative, and the intense promotion of tourism created new growth poles. The evidence suggests that these emerged as alternatives to primate cities for the migration of both workers and firms. A growth in suburbanization has also had the effect of decentralizing some of the population in the primate cities of the Caribbean, while adding to the broader metropolitan areas of these cities. The effect of these trends can be seen clearly in Jamaica, for instance, where the primacy index declined from 7.2 in 1960 to 2.2 in 1990, largely as a result of the development of the tourist industry on the northern coast of the island, the revival of bauxite production for export in the interior, and the growth of satellite cities at the edges of the broader Kingston metropolitan area.

In some Caribbean countries, however, the new growth poles have had the opposite effect. Thus, in Costa Rica, a country with a far more balanced urban system, the promotion of export manufacturing and tourism has tended to concentrate activities in the metropolitan area of the primate city of San Jose and its immediate surrounding cities, such as Cartago. Finally, in the case of Guatemala, export manufacturing and tourism are far less developed, largely because of the extremely violent political situa-

---

1. See also the special case of border cities such as Tijuana, which have exploded in growth because of the internationalization of production in the Mexico-U.S. border region and have become major destinations for migrants (Sanchez & Alegria 1992). The new export manufacturing zones in China have drawn large numbers of migrants from many regions of the country (Sklair 1985; Solinger 1999:277-90).

2. This region is here defined as consisting of the island nations between the Florida peninsula and the north coast of South America, and the independent countries of the Central American isthmus; it excludes the large nations bordering on the Caribbean Sea.

EXHIBIT 3.5

Foreign Direct Investment Inflows in Select Latin American
Countries, 1986 and 1997 (US$ millions)

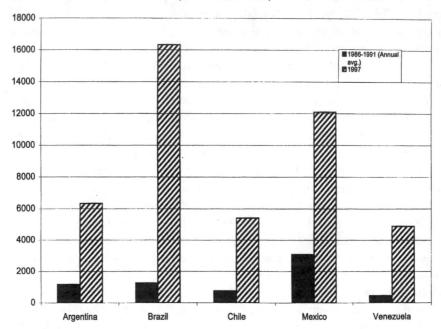

Source: Based on UNCTD, *World Investment Report 1998: Trends and Determinants*,
pp. 364-365.

tion (Jonas 1992). Development of export-oriented growth is still centered
in agriculture. Guatemala has one of the highest levels of urban primacy
in Latin America because almost no cities in that country have functioned
as growth poles. Only recently have efforts to develop export agriculture
promoted some growth in intermediate cities; thus, we see that coffee and
cotton centers have grown more rapidly than the capital, Guatemala City.

The growth of foreign direct investment since 1991 has further
strengthened the role of the major Latin American business centers, particularly Mexico City, São Paulo, and Buenos Aires (see Exhibit 3.5). As we
saw in Chapter 2, privatization has been a key component of this growth.
Foreign direct investment, via both privatization and other channels, has
been associated with deregulation of financial markets and key economic
institutions. Thus, the central role played by the stock market and other financial markets in these increasingly complex investment processes has
raised the economic importance of the major cities where these institutions are concentrated. Because the bulk of the value of investment in pri-

vatized enterprises and other, often related, investments has been in Mexico, Argentina, and Brazil, the impact of vast capital inflows is particularly felt in the corporate and financial sectors in Mexico City, Buenos Aires, and São Paulo.[3] We see in these cities the emergence of conditions that resemble patterns evident in major Western cities: highly dynamic financial markets and specialized service sectors; the **overvalorization** of the output, firms, and workers in these sectors; and the **devalorization** of the rest of the economic system. This is a subject we will return to in Chapter 4.

In brief, economic globalization has had a range of impacts on cities and urban systems in Latin America and the Caribbean. In some cases, it has contributed to the development of new growth poles outside the major urban agglomerations: This has often been the case with the development of export manufacturing zones, agriculture for export, and tourism. In others, it has actually raised the weight of primate urban agglomerations, in that the new growth poles were developed in these areas. A third case is that represented by the major business and financial centers in the region, several of which saw a sharp strengthening in their linkages with global markets and with the major international business centers in the developed world (Sassen, 2000).

Production zones, centers for tourism, and major business and financial centers are three types of sites for the implantation of global processes. Beyond these sites is a vast terrain containing cities, towns, and villages that is increasingly unhinged from this new international growth dynamic. Again, this dissociation is not simply a question of city size, since there are long subcontracting chains connecting workers in small villages to the world markets. It is, rather, a question of how these emergent transnational economic systems are articulated, how they connect specific localities in less developed countries with markets and localities in highly developed countries (see, e.g., Beneria 1989; Bonacich et al. 1994; Bose and Acosta-Belen 1995; Chaney and Castro 1993; Ward 1990). The implantation of global processes seems to have contributed to increasing the separation, or disarticulation, between cities and sectors within cities that are articulated with the global economy and those that are not. This is a new type of interurban inequality, one not predicated on old hierarchies of city size. The new inequality differs from the long-standing forms of inequality present in cities and national urban systems because of the extent to which it results from the *implantation* of a global dynamic, be it the internationalization of production and finance or international tourism.

---

3. There are several new excellent global city analyses of these cities (Ciccolella 1998; Mignaqui 1998; Schiffer 2000).

Impacts on Balanced Urban Systems: The Case of Europe

A major multiyear, multicountry study on cities in Europe, sponsored by the European Economic Community (EEC), had as one of its most interesting findings the renewed demographic and economic importance of Europe's large cities. (For a summary, see European Institute of Urban Affairs 1992, and Kunzmann and Wegener 1991; see also Eurocities 1989.) In the 1960s and 1970s, most if not all of these large cities had experienced declines in population and in economic activity, whereas smaller cities experienced growth in both dimensions. We saw a similar pattern in the United States, where this process took the form of suburbanization.

Many analysts both in Europe and in the United States asserted that central cities, with the exception of old historical centers with cultural importance, had lost much of their use to people and to the economy. The widespread growth of small cities in Europe in those two earlier decades was seen as a strong indication of how balanced the urban systems of Western European nations were and continue to be. And, indeed, compared with almost any other major continental region, Western European nations had and continue to have the most balanced urban systems in the world. Nonetheless, it is now clear that in the 1980s, and especially in the second half of that decade, major cities in Europe began to gain population and saw significant economic growth (see Exhibit 3.6). The exceptions were some of Europe's large cities in more peripheral areas: There were continuing losses in Marseilles, Naples, and England's old industrial cities, Manchester and Birmingham. Similarly, the rate of growth of smaller cities slowed down, often markedly.

These trends can be interpreted in several ways. On one hand, it could be argued that we are seeing mild demographic shifts that leave the characteristics of the urban system basically unaltered; that is, at the levels both of the nation and of Western Europe as a whole, we see balanced urban systems. On the other hand, it could be argued that we are seeing a renewed importance of major cities because the economic changes evident in all developed countries have organizational and spatial implications for such cities. The EEC study referred to earlier found that the second of these interpretations fits the data gathered for 24 cities in Europe. The evidence shows clearly that the period 1985 to 1990 marks the crucial turnaround from negative to positive population growth in the urban core after consistent losses in the preceding periods (see Exhibit 3.6; see also Eurocities 1989).

EXHIBIT 3.6

Population Change in Select European Cities, Selected Periods, 1970 to 1990

Core City[a]	1970–1975		1975–1980		1980–1985		1985–1990	
	Core	Ring	Core	Ring	Core	Ring	Core	Ring
Hamburg	-0.77	0.85	-0.91	0.36	-0.77	0.06	0.24	0.06
Frankfurt	—	—	—	—	-1.01	-0.04	1.62	0.11
Dortmund	-0.41	0.08	-0.79	-0.27	-1.15	-0.56	0.54	0.37
Berlin (West)	-1.14	0	-1.17	0	-0.49	0	2.52	0
Paris	-1.48	1.93	-0.69	0.66	-1.02	0.78	1.01	2.06
Lyons	-1.79	4.25	-1.23	1.18	0.07	-0.04	0.07	1.21
Marseilles	0.27	4.47	-0.48	2.91	-1.10	1.57	-1.10	2.84
Milan	-0.14	1.06	-1.17	1.07	-2.02	0.6	-1.03	0.35
Amsterdam	-1.84	1.51	-1.11	0.81	-1.18	0.57	0.34	0.47
Rotterdam	-1.99	1.1	-1.38	0.81	-0.28	0.56	0.22	0.28
Brussels	-1.99	0.48	-1.38	0.15	-0.95	0.02	-0.17	0.04
London	-1.89	-0.37	-1.6	-0.14	-0.38	-0.06	0.56	-0.32
Birmingham	-0.3	0.35	-1.01	-0.66	-0.33	0	-0.37	0.06
Glasgow	-3.38	-1.47	-1.84	-0.11	-1.06	-0.17	-1.41	-0.32
Dublin	-0.41	—	-0.41	—	-1.61	—	—	—
Copenhagen	-2.28	2	-1.47	0.46	-0.59	-0.12	-0.72	0.14
Thessaloniki	2.06	—	1.44	—	0.93	0.54	—	—
Athens	1.09	—	-0.16	—	-1.43	1.45	—	—
Madrid	0.45	8.28	-0.2	8.19	-0.63	3.16	0.28	0.07
Barcelona	-0.07	3.4	0.13	2.27	-0.58	0.71	0.04	-0.04
Valencia	1.44	1.47	1.11	1.73	-0.41	1.26	0.6	-0.48
Seville	1.24	-0.02	1.81	1.23	0.16	1.19	0.75	0.52
Berlin (East)	0.21	-0.05	1.14	0.14	0.9	0.06	1.85	0.17

a. Core City refers to cities in growth or dynamic regions in Western Europe.

Source: Based on A Report to the Commission of the European Communities, Directorate General for Regional Policy (SVI), April 1992, p. 56.

EXHIBIT 3.7

Select Cities in Europe, 1990

Source: Based on European Institute of Urban Affairs, *Urbanisation and the Functions of Cities in the European Community: A Report to the Commission of the European Communities, Directorate General for Regional Policy (XVI)* (1992:56).

The organizational and spatial implications of the new economic trends assume distinct forms in various urban systems. Some cities become part of transnational networks, whereas others become unhinged from the main centers of economic growth in their regions or nations. A review of the EEC report, as well as other major studies on cities in Europe, suggests that we can identify at least three tendencies in the reconfiguration of urban systems in Western Europe. First, several sub-European regional systems have emerged (European Conference of Ministers Responsible for Regional Planning (CEMAT) 1988; Kunzmann and Wegener 1991). Second, within the territory of the European Economic Community and several immediately adjacent nations (Austria, Denmark, Greece), a limited number of cities have strengthened their role in an emergent Euro-

EXHIBIT 3.8

Location of Top Banking, Industrial, and Commercial Firms, by City, Selected Years, 1960 to 1997

City, Country[a]	1997	1990	1980	1970	1960
Tokyo, Japan	18 (5)[b]	12 (2)	6	5 (1)	1
New York, USA	12 (1)	7 (5)	10 (4)	25 (8)	29 (8)
Paris, France	11 (1)	5	7 (2)	0	0
Osaka, Japan	7 (3)	2 (1)	1	1	0
Detroit, USA	4 (2)	2 (2)	2 (2)	3 (3)	5 (2)
London, UK	3 (1)	7 (2)	8 (3)	7 (3)	7 (3)
Chicago, USA	3	2	4 (2)	5	6 (2)
Munich, Germany	3	2	1	1	1
Amsterdam, Netherlands	3	0	0	0	0
Seoul, South Korea	3	0	0	0	0

a. After ranking cities according to the number holding the world's 100 largest corporation headquarters, the list was trimmed to the top 40 cities of which 10 are listed in the table above.

b. The figure in parentheses gives the number of the world's top 20 corporations for that city.

Source: Short and Kim, *Globalization and the City* (1999:26).

pean urban system. Finally, a few of these cities are also part of an urban system that operates at the global level.

The urban system within European nations is also being affected by these developments. The traditional national urban networks are changing. Cities that were once dominant in their nation may lose that importance, while cities in border regions or transportation hubs may gain a new importance. Furthermore, the new European global cities may capture some of the business, demands for specialized services, and investments that previously went to national capitals or major provincial cities. Cities at the periphery will feel the widening gap with the newly defined and positioned geography of centrality.

Cities in peripheral regions and old port cities have basically lost ground in their national urban systems as a result of the new hierarchies (Castells 1989; Hausserman and Siebel 1987; Parkinson, Foley, and Judd 1989; Roncayolo 1990; Siebel 1984; van den Berg et al. 1982; Vidal, Viard, et al., 1990). By the late 1980s, it had become clear that many had become increasingly disconnected from the major European urban systems. Some of these peripheralized cities with outmoded industrial bases have reemerged with new functions and as part of new networks in the 1990s—for example, Lille in France and Glasgow in the United Kingdom. Others have lost politico-economic functions and are unlikely to regain them in the foreseeable future. Yet others are becoming centers for tourism or places for second homes. A growing number of high-income Germans and English, for example, have bought country houses and "castles" in Ireland; other continental Europeans are following their example. Much of the beauty of the Irish countryside—whole regions untouched by industrialization—is a legacy of poverty, which may be undermined by Ireland's rapid growth. The requirement for becoming transnational centers for tourism and second homes is that these sites cannot pursue industrial development and need to preserve high levels of environmental quality.

Furthermore, changes in defense policies resulting from changes in the East will cause decline in cities that were once crucial production centers or control centers in national defense systems. Smaller port cities, or large ones that have not upgraded and modernized their infrastructures, will be at a great disadvantage in competing with the large, modernized port cities in Europe. Marseilles was once a great port, strategically located on the Mediterranean; today, it has been left behind by Rotterdam and a few other major European ports that constitute a cluster of state-of-the-art ports. Nothing in the near future seems to secure the revitalization of old industrial centers on the basis of the industries that once were their economic core. The most difficult cases are small- and medium-size cities in somewhat isolated or peripheral areas dependent on coal and steel industries. They are likely to have degraded their environments and hence do not even have the option of becoming tourist centers.

Kunzmann and Wegener (1991) see the dominance of the large cities continuing in part because the competition among cities in Europe for both European and non-European investment will continue to favor the larger high-tech industrial and service cities (see also Deecke, Kruger, and Lapple 1993). Furthermore, this spatial polarization will deepen because of the development of high-speed transport infrastructure and communications corridors, which will tend to connect major centers or highly specialized centers essential to the advanced economic system (Castells and Hall 1994; Graham and Marvin 1996; Masser, Sviden, and Wegener 1990). For example, Lille's position in the center of Western Europe has strengthened its role as a transportation and communications hub, and this once-dying industrial city is now the site of massive infrastructure projects.

We may be seeing a process of recentralization in certain cities that have been somewhat peripheral. Some of the smaller cities in Europe (such as Aachen, Strasbourg, Nice, Liege, Arnheim) are likely to benefit from the single European market insofar as they can expand their hinterland and function as a nexus to a broader European region. Changes in Eastern Europe are likely to strengthen the role of Western European cities

EXHIBIT 3.9

Foreign Direct Investment in Central and Eastern Europe, 1992 and 1997 (selected countries)

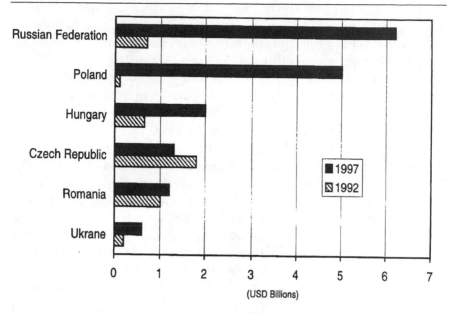

(USD Billions)

Source: Based on UNCTD, *World Investment Report* (1998:364–65).

that used to have extensive interregional linkages before World War II—notably Hamburg, Copenhagen, and Nuremberg—which in turn may have the effect of weakening the position of other peripheral cities in those regions. Cities bordering Eastern Europe may assume new roles or recapture old ones; Vienna and Berlin are emerging as international business platforms for the whole central European region.[4]

Finally, major Eastern European cities such as Budapest, Prague, and Warsaw may regain some of their prewar importance. Budapest is a good example: Toward the late 1980s, it emerged as the leading international business center for the Eastern European region, a role illustrated by the

---

4. The strengthening of Berlin, both through reunification and regaining the role of capital, may alter some of the power relations between Budapest, Vienna, and Berlin. Many analysts believe that Berlin will become the major international business center for Central Europe, with corresponding reductions in the roles of Budapest and Vienna. One could also posit that these three cities may create a regional transnational urban system for the whole region, in which both competition *and* a division of functions have the effect of strengthening the overall international business capability of the region.

fact that Hungary was the major recipient of foreign direct investment in Eastern Europe (see Exhibit 3.9) (Bodnar 1998). Although the absolute investment levels were lower than those in the former USSR (with an immensely larger territory and economy than Hungary), in relative terms, these figures represent a sharper internationalization than in the former USSR. Western European and non-European firms seeking to do business in Eastern Europe located offices in Budapest to launch operations for the region. By the early 1990s, Budapest had a rather glamorous Western-looking international business enclave that offered the requisite comforts, hotels, restaurants, and business services in a way that most other major Eastern European cities did not at the time.

Immigration is expected to grow and become a major fact in many European cities, a subject discussed in Chapter 5 (Balbo and Manconi 1990; Brown 1984; Canevari 1991; Cohen 1987; Gillette and Sayad 1984; Sassen 1999; SOPEMI [Systeme d'observation permanente pour les migrations] 1999; Tribalat et al. 1991).[5] Cities that function as gateways into Europe will receive growing immigration flows from Eastern Europe, Africa, and the Middle East. Many of these cities, particularly old port cities such as Marseilles, Palermo, and Naples, are already experiencing economic decline and will be unable to absorb the additional labor and costs (Mingione 1991). Although these cities may function largely as entrepôts, with variable shares of immigrants expected to move on to more dynamic cities, there will nonetheless be a tendency for resident immigrant populations to grow.

Having their infrastructures and services overburdened will further peripheralize these gateway cities in terms of the urban hierarchy connecting the leading cities in Europe and further contribute to polarization. On the other hand, some of Europe's global cities, such as Paris and Frankfurt, which are at the center of major transportation networks, are final destinations for many immigrants and have significant numbers in their populations and workforces (Blaschke and Germershausen 1989; Body-Gendrot, Ma Mung, and Hodier 1992; Gillette and Sayad 1984). Berlin, which according to some is an emerging global city, is also the preferred destination of many new migrations, as is Vienna. In the past, Berlin and Vienna were centers of vast regional migration systems, and they seem to be recapturing that old role. Smaller gateway cities such as

---

5. This is not an exceptional situation. All developed countries in the world now have immigrant workers. Even Japan, a country known for its anti-immigration stance, now has legal and illegal immigration, a first in its history (AMPO 1988; Asian Women's Association 1988; Iyotani 1989; Morita & Sassen 1994; Sassen 1998:chap. 4).

Thessaloniki and Trieste seem to function more narrowly as transition posts and do not appear to be as overwhelmed as some of the other, larger gateway cities.

There are, then, a multiplicity of geographies of centers and margins in Europe at this time. A central urban hierarchy connects major cities, many of which in turn play central roles in the wider global system of cities: Paris, London, Frankfurt, Amsterdam, Zurich. Somewhat less oriented to the global economy is a major network of European financial/cultural/service capitals, some with only one, others with several of these functions, which articulate the European region. And then there are several geographies of margins: the East-West divide and the North-South divide across Europe as well as new divisions. In Eastern Europe, certain cities and regions are rather attractive for purposes of both European and non-European investment, whereas others will increasingly fall behind (notably, those in Rumania, the former Yugoslavia, and Albania). We see a similar differentiation in the south of Europe: Madrid, Barcelona, and Milan are gaining in the new European hierarchy; Naples and Marseilles are not.

Transnational Urban Systems[6]

A rapidly growing and highly specialized research literature is focusing on different types of economic linkages that bind cities across national borders (Castells 1989; Daniels 1991; GaWC 1998; Graham and Marvin 1996; Leyshon, Daniels, and Thrift 1987; Noyelle and Dutka 1988; Sassen 1991, 2000). Prime examples of such linkages are the multinational networks of affiliates and subsidiaries typical of major firms in manufacturing and specialized services. The internationalization and deregulation of various financial markets is yet another, very recent development that binds cities across borders. This phenomenon is illustrated by the increasing numbers of stock markets around the world that are now participating in a global equities market. There is also a growing number of less directly economic linkages, notable among which are a variety of initiatives launched by urban governments that amount to a type of foreign policy by and for cities. In this context, the long-standing tradition of designating sister cities that has recently seen sharp growth (Zelinsky 1991) can assume a whole new meaning in the case of cities eager to operate interna-

---

6. See also the section, "Why Do We Need Financial Centers in the Global Digital Era?" in Chapter 5.

EXHIBIT 3.10a

Cities with Major Levels of Banking/Finance Links to London (number of firms, 1998)

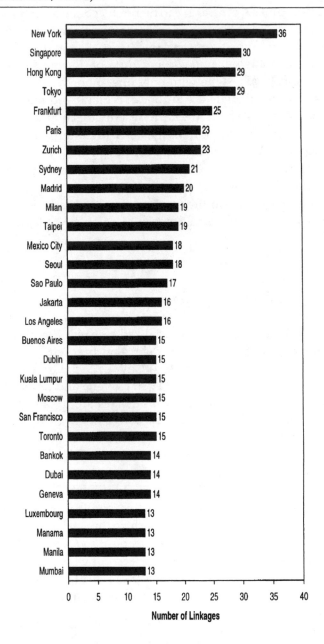

City	Number of Linkages
New York	36
Singapore	30
Hong Kong	29
Tokyo	29
Frankfurt	25
Paris	23
Zurich	23
Sydney	21
Madrid	20
Milan	19
Taipei	19
Mexico City	18
Seoul	18
Sao Paulo	17
Jakarta	16
Los Angeles	16
Buenos Aires	15
Dublin	15
Kuala Lumpur	15
Moscow	15
San Francisco	15
Toronto	15
Bankok	14
Dubai	14
Geneva	14
Luxembourg	13
Manama	13
Manila	13
Mumbai	13

Number of Linkages

EXHIBIT 3.10b

Cities with Major Levels of Law Firm Links to London, 1998 (number of firms)

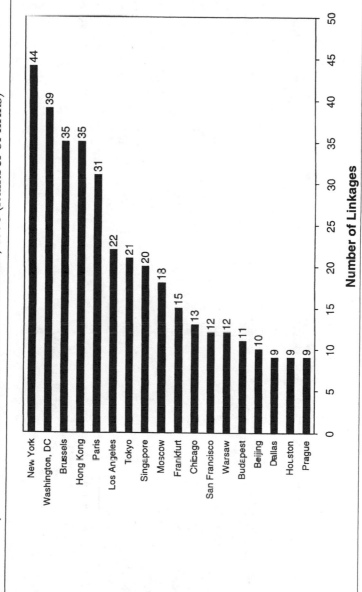

Note: Number of links denotes number of branch offices that the city or cities share with London–based firms.

Source: Based on Taylor, Walker, and Beaverstock, "Introducing GaWC" (2000).

EXHIBIT 3.11

Intrafirm Service Networks among Top Business Centers, 1998 (probabilities in percentages)

Linkage from	Chicago	Frankfurt	Hong Kong	London	Los Angeles	Milan	New York	Paris	Singapore	Tokyo
					Linkage to					
Chicago	—	89	89	100	91	79	100	89	83	100
Frankfurt	67	—	93	100	72	87	100	95	94	95
Hong Kong	60	82	—	100	80	80	100	85	92	90
London	59	77	87	—	78	78	98	83	83	86
Los Angeles	67	73	89	100	—	70	97	84	81	89
Milan	59	88	93	100	67	—	100	88	91	93
New York	59	77	87	98	77	77	—	79	83	85
Paris	64	85	90	100	80	81	97	—	90	90
Singapore	60	87	98	100	78	83	100	92	—	95
Tokyo	64	84	93	100	83	81	100	87	88	—

Note: The table is an asymmetric matrix showing probabilities of connections between cities; each cell contains the percentage probability that a firm in City X will have an office in City Y.

Source: Taylor, Walker, and Beaverstock, "Introducing GaWC" (2000:Table 14).

tionally without going through their national governments (Eurocities 1989; Sassen 2000).

Some of the most detailed data on transnational linkages binding cities come from studies on corporate service firms. Such firms have developed vast multinational networks containing special geographic and institutional linkages that make it possible for client firms—transnational firms and banks—to use a growing array of service offerings from the same supplier (Daniels 1991; Leyshon et al. 1987; Noyelle & Dutka 1988). One of the best data sets at this time on the global networks of affiliates of leading firms in finance, accounting, law, and advertising is GaWC (Globalization and World Cities Study Group and Network) (GaWC 1998; see also Sassen 2000). There is good evidence that the development of transnational corporate service firms was associated with the needs of transnational firms. Based on recent GaWC research (Globalization and World Cities Research Group and Network), the network of affiliates in banking/finance and law firms closely follows the relative importance of world cities in those two sectors (see Exhibits 3.10a and 3.10b). The transnational banking/finance or law firm, therefore, can offer global finance and legal services to a specific segment of potential customers worldwide. Furthermore, global integration of affiliates and markets requires making use of advanced information and telecommunications technology that can come to account for a significant share of costs—not just operational costs but also, and perhaps most important, research and development costs for new products or advances on existing products. This is illustrated in Exhibit 3.11, which shows the probability that firms with offices in one of the listed cities will have a branch office or affiliate in another city.

The need for scale economies on all these fronts helps explain the recent increase in mergers and acquisitions, which has consolidated the position of a few very large firms in many of these industries and has further strengthened cross-border linkages between the key locations that concentrate the needed telecommunications facilities. These few have emerged as firms that can control a significant share of national and international markets. The rapid increase in foreign direct investment in services is strongly linked with the high level of concentration in many of these industries and a strong tendency during the 1970s toward increasing market share among the larger firms. This is particularly true for firms servicing large corporations. Subcontracting by larger firms and the multiplicity of specialized markets has meant that small independent firms can also thrive in major business centers. The link between international law firms and financial firms has contributed to a centralization of law firms in major financial centers (Parkinson et al. 1989; Sassen 1991; Stanback and Noyelle 1982; see also Lash and Urry 1987).

Whether these links have engendered transnational urban systems is less clear, and is partly a question of theory and conceptualization. So much of social science is profoundly rooted in the nation-state as the ultimate unit for analysis that conceptualizing processes and systems as transnational is bound to create much controversy. Even much of the literature on world or global cities does not necessarily proclaim the existence of a transnational urban system: In its narrowest form, this literature posits that global cities perform central place functions at a transnational level. But that leaves open the question of the nature of the articulation between global cities. If we accept that they basically compete with each other for global business, then they do not constitute a transnational system. Studying several global cities then falls into the category of traditional comparative analysis. If we posit that, in addition to competing with each other, global cities are also the sites where transnational processes with multiple locations occur, then we can begin to explore the possibility of a systemic dynamic binding these cities.

Elsewhere (Sassen 1991:chaps. 1 and 7, 1999, 2000), I have argued that, in addition to the central place functions performed by these cities at the global level as posited by Hall (1966), Friedmann and Wolff (1982), and Sassen-Koob (1982), these cities relate to one another in distinct systemic ways. For example, the interactions between New York, London, and Tokyo, particularly in terms of finance and investment, consist partly of a series of processes that can be thought of as the "chain of production" in finance. Thus, in the mid-1980s, Tokyo was the main exporter of the raw material we call money, while New York was the leading processing center in the world. It was in New York that many of the new financial instruments were invented and that money either in its raw form or in the form of debt was transformed into instruments aimed at maximizing the returns on that money. London, on the other hand, was a major entrepôt that had the network to centralize and concentrate small amounts of capital available in a large number of smaller financial markets around the world, partly as a function of its older network for the administration of the British Empire (see Exhibit 3.12).

This is just one example suggesting that these cities do not simply compete with each other for the same business. There is an economic system that rests on distinct types of locations and specializations each city represents. Furthermore, it seems likely that the strengthening of transnational ties between the leading financial and business centers is accompanied by a weakening of the linkages between each of these cities and its

EXHIBIT 3.12

Top Five Global Command Centers Based on Corporations, Banks, Stock Markets, and Advertising Agencies Rankings, 1996 and 1997

Rank	City[a]	Corporations (1997)	Banks (1996)	Stock Markets (1996)[b]	Advertising Agencies (1997)
1	Tokyo	1	1	3	2
2	New York	2	6	2	1
3	London	6	4	1	3
4	Paris	3	2	5	5
5	Frankfurt	11	3	4	11

a. Cities ranked within the top 20 in the corporation (based on *Fortune's* Global 500) and bank tables, within the top 5 stock markets and within the top 17 advertising agencies.

b. Based on the number of listed companies (domestic and foreign).

Source: Short and Kim, *Globalization and the City* (1999:36).

hinterland and national urban system (Sassen 1991). Cities such as Detroit, Liverpool, Manchester, Marseilles, the cities of the Ruhr, and now increasingly Nagoya and Osaka have been affected by the territorial decentralization of many of their key manufacturing industries at the domestic and international level. This process of decentralization has contributed to the growth of service industries that produce the specialized inputs to run spatially dispersed production processes and global markets for inputs and outputs. In a representative case, General Motors, whose main offices are in Detroit, also has a headquarters in Manhattan that does all the specialized financial work this vast multinational firm requires. Such specialized inputs—international legal and accounting services, management consulting, financial services—are heavily concentrated in business and financial centers rather than in manufacturing cities.

Conclusion: Urban Growth and Its Multiple Meanings

Major recent developments in urban systems point to several trends. In the developing world, we see the continuing growth of megacities and primacy as well as the emergence of new growth poles resulting from the internationalization of production and the development of tourism. In some cases, these new growth poles emerge as new destinations for migrants and thereby contribute to a deceleration in primacy; in other cases, when they are located in a primate city's area, they have the opposite effect.

In the developed world, and particularly in Western Europe, we see the renewed strength of major cities that appear to concentrate a significant and often disproportionate share of economic activity in leading sectors. In the 1970s, many of the major cities in highly developed countries were losing population and economic activity. Much was said at the time about the irreversible decline of these cities. But beginning in the mid-1980s, there has been a resurgence that results in good part from the intersection of two major trends: (1) the shift to services, most particularly the ascendance of finance and specialized services in all advanced economies, and (2) the increasing transnationalization of economic activity. This transnationalization can operate at the regional, continental, or global level. These two trends are interlinked and feed on each other. The spatial implications are a strong tendency toward agglomeration of the pertinent activities in major cities. This dynamic of urban growth is based largely on the locational needs or preferences of firms and does not necessarily compensate for population losses to suburbanization. Urban growth in less developed countries, by contrast, results largely from population growth, especially in-migration.

The transnationalization of economic activity has raised the intensity and volume of transaction between cities; whether this has contributed to the formation of transnational global urban systems is a question that requires more research. The growth of global markets for finance and specialized services, the need for transnational servicing networks in response to sharp increases in international investment, the reduced role of the government in the regulation of international economic activity and the corresponding ascendance of other institutional arenas, notably global markets and corporate headquarters—all these point to the existence of transnational economic arrangements with multiple locations in more than one country. We can see here the formation, at least an incipient one, of a transnational urban system.

The pronounced orientation to the world markets evident in such cities raises questions about the articulation with their hinterlands and nation-states. Cities typically have been and still are deeply embedded in the economies of their region, indeed often reflecting the characteristics of the latter. But cities that are strategic sites in the global economy tend, in part, to disconnect from their region. This phenomenon also conflicts with a key proposition in traditional scholarship about urban systems—namely, that these systems promote the territorial integration of regional and national economies.

Two tendencies contributing to new forms of inequality among cities are visible in the geography and characteristics of urban systems. On one hand, there is growing articulation at a transnational level among cities. This is evident both at a regional transnational level and at the global level; in some cases, there are what one could think of as overlapping geographies of articulation or overlapping hierarchies that operate at more than one level; that is to say, there are cities such as Paris or London that belong to a national urban system or hierarchy, to a transnational European system, and to a global system. On the other hand, cities and areas outside these hierarchies tend to become peripheralized, or become more so than they had been.

4

The New Urban Economy
The Intersection of Global Processes and Place

How are the management, financing, and servicing processes of internationalization actually constituted in cities that function as regional or global nodes in the world economy? And what is the work in terms of command functions and servicing operations at the world scale that gets done in cities?

To understand the new or sharply expanded role of a particular kind of city in the world economy since the early 1980s, we need to focus on the intersection of two major processes. The first process is the sharp growth in the globalization of economic activity discussed in Chapter 2. This economic globalization has raised the scale and the complexity of international transactions, thereby feeding the growth of top-level multinational headquarters functions and the growth of services for firms, particularly advanced corporate services. It is important to note that even though globalization raises the scale and complexity of these operations, they are also evident at smaller geographic scales and lower orders of complexity (such as firms that operate regionally). Thus, although such regionally oriented firms need not negotiate the complexities of international borders and the regulations of different countries, they are still faced with a regionally dispersed network of operations that requires centralized control and servicing.

The second process we need to consider is the growing service intensity in the organization of all industries (see Sassen 1991:chap. 5). This development has contributed to a massive growth in the demand for services by firms in all industries, from mining and manufacturing to finance and consumer services. Cities are key sites for the production of services for firms. Hence, the increase in service intensity in the organization of all industries has had a significant growth effect on cities beginning in the 1980s. It is important to recognize that this growth in services for firms is evident in cities at different levels of a nation's urban system. Some of these cities cater to regional or subnational markets, others cater to national markets, and yet others cater to global markets. In this context, globalization becomes a question of scale and added complexity.

The key process from the perspective of the urban economy, however, is the growing demand for services by firms in all industries and the fact that cities are preferred production sites for such services, whether at the global, national, or regional level. As a result, we see in cities the formation of a new urban economic core of banking and service activities that comes to replace the older, typically manufacturing-oriented office core.

In the case of cities that are major international business centers, the scale, power, and profit levels of this new core suggest that we are seeing the formation of a new urban economy. This is so in at least two regards. First, even though these cities have long been centers for business and finance, since the mid-1980s there have been dramatic changes in the structure of the business and financial sectors, as well as sharp increases in the overall magnitude of these sectors and their weight in the urban economy. Second, the ascendance of the new finance and services complex, particularly in international finance, engenders what may be regarded as a new economic regime; that is, although this sector may account for only a fraction of the economy of a city, it imposes itself on that larger economy. Most notably, the possibility for superprofits in finance has the effect of devalorizing manufacturing insofar as the latter cannot generate the superprofits typical in much financial activity.

This is not to say that everything in the economy of these cities has changed. On the contrary, they still show a great deal of continuity and many similarities with cities that are not global nodes. Rather, the implantation of global processes and markets has meant that the internationalized sector of the economy has expanded sharply and has imposed a new **valorization** dynamic—that is, a new set of criteria for valuing or pricing various economic activities and outcomes. This has had devastating effects on large sectors of the urban economy. High prices and profit levels in the internationalized sector and its ancillary activities, such as top-of-the-line restaurants and hotels, have made it increasingly difficult for other sectors to compete for space and investments. Many of these other sectors have experienced considerable downgrading and/or displacement; for example, neighborhood shops tailored to local needs are replaced by upscale boutiques and restaurants catering to the new high-income urban elite.

Although at a different order of magnitude, these trends also became evident during the late 1980s in a number of major cities in the developing world that have become integrated into various world markets: São Paulo, Buenos Aires, Bangkok, Taipei, and Mexico City are only a few examples. Also in these cities, the new urban core was fed by the deregulation of financial markets, the ascendance of finance and specialized services, and integration into the world markets. The opening of stock markets to foreign investors and the privatization of what were once public sector firms have been crucial institutional arenas for this articulation. Given the vast size of some of these cities, the impact of this new core on the broader city is not always as evident as in central London or Frankfurt, but the transformation is still very real.

In this chapter, we will examine the characteristics of the new dominant sector in the urban economy of highly internationalized cities. We begin with a discussion of producer services, the core sector of the new urban economy, and the conditions shaping the growth and locational patterns of these services. We then turn to the formation of a new producer services complex in major cities, using the coordination and planning requirements of large transnational corporations as a working example of some of these issues. We also examine the locational patterns of major headquarters as a way to understand the significance of headquarters concentration in cities. We conclude with a look at the impact of the international financial and real estate crisis beginning at the end of the 1980s on the urban economy.

Producer Services

The expansion of producer services is a central feature of current growth in developed countries. In country after country, we see a decline or slowdown in manufacturing alongside sharp growth in producer services. Elsewhere, I have posited that the fundamental reason for this growth lies in the increased service intensity in the organization of all industries (Sassen 1991:166-68). Whether in manufacturing or in warehousing, firms are using more legal, financial, advertising, consulting, and accounting services. These services can be seen as part of the supply capacity of an economy because they facilitate adjustments to changing economic circumstances (Marshall et al. 1986:16). They are a mechanism that "organizes and adjudicates economic exchange for a fee" (Thrift 1987) and are part of a broader intermediary space of economic activity.

Producer services are services for firms. They include financial, legal, and general management matters; innovation; development; design; administration; personnel; production technology; maintenance; transport; communications; wholesale distribution; advertising; cleaning services for firms; security; and storage. Central components of the producer services category are a range of industries with mixed business and consumer markets. They are insurance, banking, financial services, real estate, legal services, accounting, and professional associations.[1]

Although disproportionately concentrated in the largest cities, producer services are actually growing at faster rates at the national level in most developed economies. The crucial process feeding the growth of producer services is the increasing use of service inputs by firms in all industries. Households have also raised their consumption of services, either directly (such as the growing use of accountants to prepare tax returns) or indirectly via the reorganization of consumer industries (buying flowers or dinner from franchises or chains rather than from self-standing and privately owned "Mom-and-Pop" shops). Services directly bought by consumers tend to be located, often as mere outlets, wherever population is concentrated. In that regard, they are far less concentrated than producer services, especially those catering to top firms. The demand for specialized services by households, from accounting to architects, may be a key factor contributing to the growth of these services at the national level.

National figures on employment trends, for the crucial period of the shift, clearly show that the producer services are the fastest growing sector in most developed economies (see Exhibit 4.1). Thus, total employment in the United States grew from 76.8 million in 1970 to 102.2 million in 1996, but producer services grew from 6.3 to 17.6 million. In this almost three-fold jump, the largest single increase was in miscellaneous business services, and the second largest was in legal services. In contrast, manufacturing grew only from 19.9 to 20.4 million. The other major growth sectors were the social services, which grew from 16.9 to 29.8 million, and personal services, from 7.7 to 13.7 million—significant levels but not nearly the rate of producer services. Distributive services also showed strong growth, from 17.2 to 24 million.

We see parallel patterns in other developed economies. Total employment in Japan grew from 52.1 million in 1970 to 65.1 million in 1998. From 1970 to 1990, producer services more than doubled from 2.5 to 5.9 million, social services from 5.4 to 8.9 million, and personal services from 4.4 to 6.3

---

1. Mixed markets create measurement problems. These problems can be partly overcome by the fact that the consumer and business markets in these industries often involve very different sets of firms and different types of location patterns, and hence, they can be distinguished on this basis. Given the existence of mixed markets and the difficulty of distinguishing between markets in the organization of the pertinent data, it is helpful to group these services under the category of "mostly" producer services—that is, services produced mostly for firms rather than for individuals. It has become customary to refer to them, for convenience, as producer services.

EXHIBIT 4.1

National Figures on Employment Trends in Three Developed Economies, 1970 and 1991 (in millions)

	Japan		Germany		United States	
	1970	*1990*	*1970*	*1987*	*1970*	*1991*
I. Extractive	10,309	4,448	2,313	1,103	3,504	4,123
Agriculture	10,087	4,383	1,991	866	2,868	3,390
Mining	222	66	323	237	636	733
II. Transformative	17,772	20,795	12,481	10,835	25,310	28,824
Construction	3,943	5,906	2,033	1,908	4,634	7,087
Utilities	288	345	215	274	811	1,303
Manufacturing	13,541	14,544	10,234	8,654	19,864	20,434
Food	1,086	1,391	964	778	1,456	1,784
Textiles	1,427	714	635	307	968	688
Metal	2,103	1,985	1,243	1,168	2,391	1,992
Machinery	2,596	3,620	2,517	1,311	3,921	4,349
Chemical	666	679	634	736	1,189	1,525
Misc. mfg.	5,664	6,155	4,240	4,353	9,940	10,096
III. Distributive services	11,689	14,987	4,748	4,765	17,190	24,079
Transportation	2,636	3,097	1,443	15,74	3,013	4,170
Communication	577	598	—	—	1,132	1,598
Wholesale	3,159	4,377	1,125	873	3,100	4,640
Retail	5,316	6,916	2,179	2,318	9,946	13,671
IV. Producer services	2,522	5,945	1,187	1,977	6,298	16,350
Banking	729	1,181	438	658	1,658	3,286
Insurance	376	783	244	257	1,406	2,419
Real estate	274	707	92	109	789	2,081
Engineering	268	509	163	198	333	833
Accounting	93	188	—	—	303	660
Misc. bus. serv.	741	2,493	250	754	1,401	5,797
Legal services	42	85	—	—	409	1,274
V. Social services	5,359	8,855	4,155	6,550	16,888	29,839
Medical, health serv.	?11	943	815	1,465	1,846	5,259
Hospital	923	1,328	—	—	2,836	4,839
Education	1,537	2,757	802	1,314	6,546	9,366
Welfare, relig. serv.	381	847	245	410	908	3,154
Nonprofit org.	524	656	112	56	330	468
Postal service	—	—	—	—	732	852
Government	1,759	2,092	2,053	2,545	3,484	5,639
Misc. social services	23	232	128	760	206	262
VI. Personal services	4,441	6,296	1,610	1,687	7,696	13,659
Domestic serv.	153	80	116	56	1,272	1,000
Hotel	463	677	730	731	731	1,813
Eating, drinking places	1,585	2,538	—	—	2,479	5,744
Repair services	480	614	271	297	1,056	1,670
Laundry	239	349	120	62	587	470
Barber, beauty shops	565	650	234	258	728	876
Entertainment	425	822	119	248	632	1,570
Misc. personal serv.	532	567	19	35	211	516
All other services	19	366	—	—	—	—
Total	52,110	61,734	26,494	26,908	76,805	116,877

Source: Based on Castells and Aoyama (1994).

million. In 1998, manufacturing dropped from 14.5 million in 1985 to 13.8 million; wholesale and retail trade increased from 13.2 to 14.8 million; all services increased from 11.7 to 16.9 million; FIRE increased from 2.2 to 2.6 million.

In France, total employment went from 20 million in 1968 to 21.8 million in 1989 to 22.7 million in 1998. From 1968 to 1989, producer and personal services doubled, while social and distributive services showed strong growth too. Manufacturing fell from 5.4 to 4.6 million. By 1998, 69.2% of employment was in the services sector.

In the United Kingdom, total employment grew from 23.4 million in 1970 to 26.9 million in 1998. Manufacturing lost almost half of its jobs, going from 9 to 4.5 million in 1992. But as in other developed economies, producer services more than doubled, from 1.2 million in 1970 to 2.6 million and social services grew from 4.2 to 6.1 million. By 1998, 71.6% of employment was in the services sector.

Finally, in Canada, total employment grew from 8.4 million in 1971 to 14.3 million in 1998. But producer services tripled from 0.5 to 1.6 million; miscellaneous business services accounted for two-thirds of this growth. From 1985 to 1998, business services alone grew from 0.6 to 1.1 million. All other service sectors also grew strongly while manufacturing fell from 2.2 to 2 million during the same period.

In the 1980s, producer services became the most dynamic, fastest-growing sector in many cities. Particularly notable here is the case of the United Kingdom, where overall employment actually fell and manufacturing suffered severe losses. Yet there were sharp increases in producer services in Central London between 1984 and 1987; their share rose from 31% to 37% of all employment, reaching 40% by 1989 (Frost and Spence 1992). Central London saw both relative and absolute declines in all other major employment sectors. Similar developments can be seen in New York City; in 1987, at the height of the 1980s boom, producer services accounted for 37.7% of private sector jobs, up from 29.8% in 1977. There were high growth rates in many of the producer services during the period when economic restructuring was consolidated in New York City: From 1977 to 1985, employment in legal services grew by 62%, in business services by 42%, and in banking by 23%; in contrast, employment fell by 22% in manufacturing and by 20% in transport. In the 1990s, national growth took off in these services and far surpassed the growth rate of the major cities.

Accompanying these sharp growth rates in producer services was an increase in the level of employment specialization in business and financial services in major cities throughout the 1980s. For example, over 90% of jobs in finance, insurance, and real estate (FIRE) in New York City were located in Manhattan, as were 85% of business service jobs. If we consider only those components of producer services that may be described as information industries, we can see a steady growth in jobs across the U.S. and in its major cities, with New York City posting a significantly higher concentration than any other major American city. From the mid-1980s to 1996, information industries grew from 31% of jobs in New York City to 45.2%, from 17.8% to 22.2% in Los Angeles (county), and from 20.3% to 26.1% in Chicago; all three cities show a higher incidence than the U.S. average, which grew from 15.1% to 19.3% (see also Fainstein 1993).

Beginning in the mid-1980s, we see a general trend toward high concentration of finance and certain producer services in the downtowns of major international financial centers around the world. From Toronto and Sydney to Frankfurt and Zurich, we are seeing growing specialization in financial districts everywhere. It is worth noting that this trend is also evident in the multipolar urban system of the United States: Against all odds, New York City has kept its place at the top in terms of concentration in banking and finance (see Exhibits 4.2, 4.3, and 4.4). By 1990, finance and business services in the New York metro area were more concentrated in Manhattan than they were in the mid-1950s (Harris 1991).[2]

These cities have emerged as important producers of services for export, with a tendency toward specialization. New York and London are leading producers and exporters in accounting, advertising, management consulting, international legal services, and other business services. In fact, New York, London, Tokyo, Paris, and Frankfurt accounted for 63.37% of the world's top 50 largest commercial bank assets in 1997 (Exhibit 4.5), and Tokyo, New York, and London alone accounted for 33.15% of the world's top 50 largest insurer assets in the same year (Exhibit 4.6) They are the most important international markets for these services, with New York the world's largest source of service exports. By the late 1980s, Tokyo emerged as an important center for the international trade in services, going beyond its initial restricted role of exporting only the services required by its large international trading houses. Japanese firms are more likely to gain a significant share of the world market in certain producer services, construction and engineering, than others, such as advertising and international legal services (Rimmer 1988). As recently as 1978, the United States accounted for 60 of the top 200 international construction contrac-

---

2. Jobs are far more concentrated in the central business district in New York City, compared with other major cities in the United States: By the late 1980s, about 27% of all jobs in the consolidated statistical area were in Manhattan, compared with 9% nationally (Drennan 1989). The 90% concentration ratio of finance is far above the norm.

EXHIBIT 4.2

U.S. Cities Ranked by Assets of 50 Largest Diversified Financial Companies, 1992 (US$ millions)

City	Assets	Percentage of U.S. Top 100
Total, Top 100 U.S. Firms	1,630,258.1	—
New York	835,461.8	51.2
Chicago	23,052.6	4.2
Metro Chicago Area	45,900.9	
Total Chicago	68,953.5	
San Francisco	38,203.0	2.3
Los Angeles	1,913.8	0.2
Total of above areas	944,532.1	57.9

Rank	City	Assets (in US$ millions)
1	New York	835,461.80
2	Washington, DC	231,977.00
3	Hartford	143,530.20
4	Philadelphia[a]	69,827.00
5	Chicago (including Metro Area)	68,953.50
6	McLean, VA[a]	59,502.00
7	Houston[a]	39,742.00
8	San Francisco	38,203.00
24	Los Angeles[a]	1,913.80

a. Denotes cities with only one company in Top 50.
Source: Based on "The Service 500," *Fortune,* May 31, 1993, pp. 199-230.

tors, and Japan for 10 (Rimmer 1988); by 1985, each accounted for 34 of such firms (see Sassen 1991:174-75). By the late 1990s, however, Japan was still importing more services than it was exporting (measuring in terms of value).

There are also tendencies toward specialization among different cities within a country. In the United States, New York leads in banking, securities, manufacturing administration, accounting, and advertising. Washington, D.C., leads in legal services, computing and data processing, management and public relations, research and development, and membership organizations. New York is more narrowly specialized as a financial, business, and cultural center. Some of the legal activity concentrated in Washington, D.C., is actually serving New York City businesses that have to go through legal and regulatory procedures, lobbying, and so on. Such services are bound to be found in the national capital, and many are oriented to the national economy and to noneconomic purposes. Furthermore, much of the research activity in Washington is aimed not at the

EXHIBIT 4.3

Cities Ranked by Assets of the World's Top 25 Largest Securities Firms, 1997 (US$ millions)

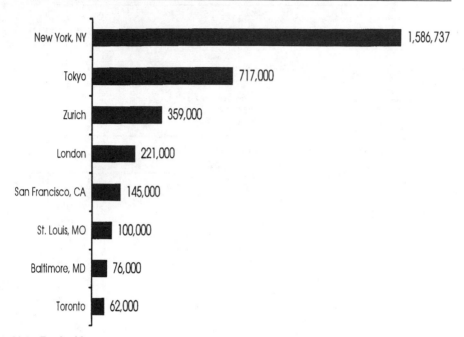

New York, NY — 1,586,737
Tokyo — 717,000
Zurich — 359,000
London — 221,000
San Francisco, CA — 145,000
St. Louis, MO — 100,000
Baltimore, MD — 76,000
Toronto — 62,000

Note: Ranked by capital as determined by Dow Jones Global Indexes; figures based on 1997 fiscal year results.

Source: Based on "World Business," *Wall Street Journal,* September 22, 1989; "World Business," *Wall Street Journal,* September 28, 1998.

world economy but at national medical and health research agendas. Thus, it is obviously important to distinguish whether a producer services complex is oriented to world markets and integration into the global economy or whether it responds largely to domestic demand.[3]

It is important to recognize that manufacturing remains a crucial sector in all of these economies, even when it may have ceased to be a domi-

---

3. The data on producer services is creating a certain amount of confusion in the United States. For example, faster growth at the national level and in medium-size cities is often interpreted as indicating a loss of share and declining position of leading centers such as New York or Chicago. Thus, one way of reading these data is as decentralization of producer services: that is, New York and Chicago are losing a share of all producer services in the United States—a zero-sum situation in which growth in a new location is construed ipso facto as a loss in an older location. Another way is to read it as growth everywhere. In my reading, the evidence points to the second type of explanation: The growing service intensity in the organization of the economy nationwide is the main factor explaining growth in medium-size cities rather than the loss of producer services firms in major cities and their relocation to other cities.

EXHIBIT 4.4

U.S. Cities Ranked by Assets of 100 Largest Commercial Banking Companies, 1992 (US$ millions)

City	Assets	Percentage of U.S. Top 100
Total, Top 100 U.S. Firms	2,500,315	—
New York	715,065	28.6
San Francisco	263,508	10.5
Chicago	109,761	4.4
Los Angeles	58,163	2.3
Total of above cities	1,146,497	45.9

Rank	City	Assets
1	New York	715,065
2	San Francisco	263,508
3	Charlotte, NC	169,386
4	Chicago	109,761
5	Pittsburgh	93,742
6	Columbus, OH	75,312
7	Minneapolis	68,084
8	Detroit	67,524
9	Boston	58,742
10	Los Angeles	58,163

Source: Based on "The Service 500," *Fortune,* May 31, 1993, pp. 199-230.

nant sector in major cities. Indeed, several scholars have argued that the producer services sector could not exist without manufacturing (Cohen and Zysman 1987; Markusen and Gwiasda 1991). In this context, it has been argued, for example, that the weakening of the manufacturing sector in the broader New York region is a threat to the city's status as a leading financial and producer services center (Markusen and Gwiasda 1991). A key proposition for this argument is that producer services depend on a strong manufacturing sector for growth. There is considerable debate around this issue (Drennan 1992; Noyelle and Dutka 1988; Sassen 1991). Drennan (1992), a leading analyst of the producer services sector in New York City, argues that a strong finance and producer services sector is possible in New York notwithstanding decline in its industrial base and that these sectors are so strongly integrated into the world markets that articulation with their hinterland—that is, integration with their regions— becomes secondary.

EXHIBIT 4.5

Cities Ranked by Assets of the World's Top 50 Largest Commercial Banks, 1997 (US$ millions)

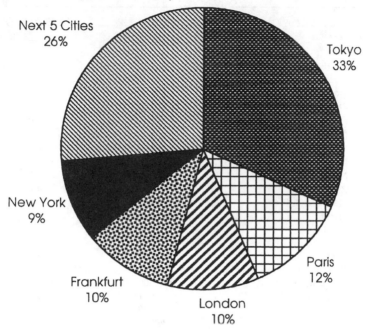

Source: Based on "World Business," *Wall Street Journal*, September 22, 1989; "World Business," *Wall Street Journal*, September 28, 1998.

In a variant on both positions (Sassen 1991), I argue that manufacturing indeed is one factor feeding the growth of the producer services sector but that it does so whether located in the area in question or overseas. Even though manufacturing—and mining and agriculture, for that matter—feeds growth in the demand for producer services, its actual location is of secondary importance for global level service firms: Thus, whether manufacturing plants are located offshore or within a country may be quite irrelevant as long as they are part of a multinational corporation likely to buy the services from top-level firms. Second, the territorial dispersal of plants, especially if international, actually raises the demand for producer services. This is yet another meaning, or consequence, of globalization: The growth of producer service firms headquartered in New York or London or Paris can be fed by manufacturing located anywhere in the world as long as it is part of a multinational corporate network. Third, a good part of the producer services sector is fed by financial and business

EXHIBIT 4.6

Cities Ranked by Assets of the World's Top 50 Largest Insurers, 1997 (US$ millions)

Rank	City	Assets	Percentage of Top 50
Total for Top 50		5,934,915	—

Top 20 Cities in the World (ranked by assets)

Rank	City	Assets	Percentage of Top 50
1	Tokyo	895,659	15.09
2	New York	543,740	9.16
3	London	527,929	8.90
4	Osaka	504,944	8.51
5	Munich	409,762	6.90
6	Paris	407,930	6.87
7	Newark, NJ	259,482	4.37
8	Zurich	238,924	4.03
9	Hartford, CT	228,275	3.85
10	Trieste	140,742	2.37
11	The Hague	134,618	2.27
12	Amsterdam	120,849	2.04
13	Boston	107,827	1.82
14	Philadelphia, PA	106,411	1.79
15	Bloomington, IN	103,600	1.75
16	Cleveland, OH	96,001	1.62
17	Edinburgh	92,888	1.57
18	Norwich, CN	86,553	1.46
19	Columbus, OH	83,214	1.40
20	Northbrook, IL	80,918	1.36

Top 10 Cities in the United States

Rank	City	Assets	Percentage of Top 50
1	New York	543,740	9.16
2	Newark, NJ	259,482	4.37
3	Hartford, CT	228,275	3.85
4	Philadelphia, PA	106,411	1.79
5	Bloomington, IN	103,600	1.75
6	Cleveland, OH	96,001	1.62
7	Columbus, OH	83,214	1.40
8	Northbrook, IL	80,918	1.36
9	Houston, TX	80,620	1.36
10	Fort Wayne, IN	77,175	1.30
Total for U.S.		1,659,436	
Percentage of World Total		27.96	

Note: Ranked by capital as determined by Dow Jones Global Indexes; figures based on 1997 fiscal year results.

Source: Based on "World Business," *Wall Street Journal*, September 22, 1989; "World Business," *Wall Street Journal*, September 28, 1998.

transactions that either have nothing to do with manufacturing, as in many of the global financial markets, or for which manufacturing is incidental, as in much merger and acquisition activity (which is centered on buying and selling firms no matter what they do).

Some of the employment figures on New York and London, two cities that experienced heavy losses in manufacturing and sharp gains in producer services, illustrate this point. New York lost 34% of its manufacturing jobs from 1969 to 1989 in a national economy that overall lost only 2% of such jobs and that actually saw manufacturing growth in many areas. The British economy lost 32% of its manufacturing jobs from 1971 to 1989, and the London region lost 47% of such jobs (Fainstein, Gordon, and Harloe 1992; Buck, Drennan, and Newton 1992). Yet both cities had sharp growth in producer services and raised the shares of such jobs in each city's total employment. Furthermore, it is also worth considering the different conditions in each city's larger region: London's region had a 2% employment decline compared with a 22% job growth rate in the larger New York region. This divergence points to the fact that the finance and producer services complex in each city rests on a growth dynamic that is somewhat independent of the broader regional economy—a sharp change from the past, when a city was presumed to be deeply articulated with its hinterland.

The Formation of a
New Production Complex

According to standard conceptions about information industries, the rapid growth and disproportionate concentration of many of the producer services in central cities should not have happened. This is especially so for advanced corporate services, because they are thoroughly embedded in the most advanced information technologies; they would seem to have locational options that bypass the high costs and congestion typical of major cities. But cities offer agglomeration economies and highly innovative environments. Some of these services are produced in-house by firms, but a large share are bought from specialized service firms. The growing complexity, diversity, and specialization of the services required makes it more efficient to buy them from specialized firms rather than hiring in-house professionals. The growing demand for these services has made possible the economic viability of a freestanding specialized service sector.

A production process takes place in these services that benefits from proximity to other specialized services. This is especially the case in the leading and most innovative sectors of these industries. Complexity and innovation often require multiple highly specialized inputs from several industries. The production of a financial instrument, for example, requires inputs from accounting, advertising, legal services, economic consulting, public relations, design, and printing. In this regard, these are highly net-worked firms. These particular characteristics of production explain the centralization of management and servicing functions that has fueled the economic boom in major cities beginning in the mid-1980s. The commonly heard explanation that high-level professionals require face-to-face interactions needs to be refined in several ways. Producer services, unlike other types of services, are not necessarily dependent on spatial proximity to buyers—that is, firms served. Rather, economies occur in such specialized firms when they locate close to others that produce key inputs or whose proximity makes possible joint production of certain service offerings. The accounting firm can service its clients at a distance, but the nature of its service depends on proximity to specialists, lawyers, and programmers. Moreover, concentration arises out of the needs and expectations of the people likely to be employed in these new high-skill jobs who tend to be attracted to the amenities and lifestyles that large urban centers can offer. Frequently, what is thought of as face-to-face communication is actually a production process that requires multiple simultaneous inputs and feedbacks. At the current stage of technical development, having immediate and simultaneous access to the pertinent experts is still the most effective way to operate, especially when dealing with a highly complex product.

Furthermore, time replaces weight in these sectors as a force for agglomeration. In the past, the pressure of the weight of inputs from iron ore to unprocessed agricultural products was a major constraint pushing toward agglomeration in sites where the heaviest inputs were located. Today, the acceleration of economic transactions and the premium put on time have created new forces for agglomeration; that is, if there were no need to hurry, the client could conceivably make use of a widely dispersed array of cooperating specialized firms. And this is often the case in routine operations. Where time is of the essence, however, as it is today in many of the leading sectors of these industries, the benefits of agglomeration are still extremely high—to the point where it is not simply a cost advantage but an indispensable arrangement. Central here has been the general acceleration of all transactions, especially in finance, where minutes and seconds count, in the stock markets, the foreign currency markets, the futures markets, and so on.

It is just this combination of constraints that has promoted the formation of a producer services complex in all major cities. This producer services complex is intimately connected to the world of corporate headquarters; they are often thought of as forming a joint headquarters-corporate services complex. But in the analysis developed in this book, we need to distinguish the two. Although it is true that headquarters still tend to be disproportionately concentrated in cities, many have moved out over the last two decades. Headquarters can indeed locate outside cities, but they need a producer services *complex* somewhere to buy or contract for the needed specialized services and financing. Headquarters of firms with very high overseas activity or in highly innovative and complex lines of business still tend to locate in major cities. In brief, firms in more routinized lines of activity, with predominantly regional or national markets, appear to be increasingly free to move or install their headquarters outside cities. Firms in highly competitive and innovative lines of activity and/or with a strong world market orientation appear to benefit from being located at the center of major international business centers, no matter how high the costs.

Both types of firms, however, need a corporate services sector complex to be located somewhere. Where this complex is located is probably becoming increasingly unimportant from the perspective of many, though not all, headquarters. However, from the perspective of producer services firms, such a specialized complex is most likely to be in a city, rather than, for example, in a suburban office park. The latter will be the site for producer services firms but not for a services complex. And only such a complex is capable of handling the most advanced and complicated corporate needs.

These issues are examined in the next two sections. The first discusses how the spatial dispersal of economic activities engenders an increased demand for specialized services; the transnational corporation is one of the major agents in this process. The second section examines whether and, if so, under what conditions corporate headquarters need cities.

The Servicing of Transnational Corporations

The sharp rise in the use of producer services has also been fed by the territorial dispersal of multi-establishment firms, whether at the regional, national, or global level. Firms operating many plants, offices, and service outlets must coordinate planning, internal administration and distribution, marketing, and other central headquarters activities. As large corporations move into the production and sale of final consumer services, a wide range of activities previously performed by freestanding consumer service firms are shifted to the central headquarters of the new corporate owners. Regional, national, or global chains of motels, food outlets, and flower shops require vast centralized administrative and servicing structures. A parallel pattern of expansion of central high-level planning and control operations takes place in governments, brought about partly by the technical developments that make this expansion possible and partly by the growing complexity of regulatory and administrative tasks.

Formally, the development of the modern corporation and its massive participation in world markets and foreign countries has made planning, internal administration, product development, and research increasingly important and complex. Diversification of product lines, mergers, and transnationalization of economic activities all require highly specialized skills. A firm with a multiplicity of geographically dispersed manufacturing plants contributes to the development of new types of planning in production and distribution surrounding the firm. The development of multisite manufacturing, service, and banking has created an expanded demand for a wide range of specialized service activities to manage and control global networks of factories, service outlets, and branch offices. Although to some extent these activities can be carried out in-house, a large share is not. High levels of specialization, the possibility of externalizing the production of some of these services, and the growing demand by large and small firms and by governments are all conditions that have both resulted from and made possible the development of a market for freestanding service firms that produce components for what might be called global control capability.

This in turn means that small firms can buy components of that capability, such as management consulting or international legal advice, and so can firms and governments from anywhere in the world. This accessibility contributes to the formation of marketplaces for such services in major cities. In brief, although the large corporation is undoubtedly a key agent inducing the development of this capability and is its prime beneficiary, it is not the sole user.

A brief examination of the territorial dispersal entailed by transnational operations of large enterprises can serve to illustrate some of the points raised here. Exhibits 4.7a and 4.7b, for example, show the portion of assets, sales, and workers that the 25 largest nonfinancial transnational corporations of the world have outside their home countries. We know furthermore that there were 36,600 transnationals operating in 1991 and more than 170,000 affiliates, and that those numbers jumped to 53,607 transnationals in 1996 and a total of almost 450,000 affiliates (Exhibit 2.4). More specifically, Exhibit 4.8 shows that the leading economies in the world have a disproportionate share of affiliates. Thus in 1990, Germany had more than 19,000 affiliates in foreign countries, up from 14,000 in 1984; the United States had almost 19,000. Calculations using the information in Exhibits 4.7a and 4.7b show that the share of foreign sales in the top 25 largest nonfinancial transnational corporations in the world grew from 37% to 58% just between 1990 and 1996. The share of foreign employment to total employment in the top corporations held steady at approximately 50%, a considerable figure given that the average workforce of these TNCs was 175,000 employees. Exhibit 4.9 shows the disproportionate concentration of the top TNCs ranked by foreign assets, in two parts of the world—the European Union, with 39 of these, and the United States, with 30. Together, these two regions account for two thirds of these firms.

What these figures show is a vast operation dispersed over a multiplicity of locations. Operations as extensive as these feed the expansion of central management, coordination, control, and servicing functions. Some of these functions are performed in the headquarters; others are bought or contracted for, thereby feeding the growth of the producer services complex.

Corporate Headquarters and Cities

It is very common in the general literature and in some more scholarly accounts to use the concentration of major headquarters as an indication of a city's status as an international business center. The loss of these types of headquarters is then interpreted as a decline in a city's status. In fact, using such headquarters concentration as an index is increasingly a problematic measure, given the way in which corporations are classified and the locational options telecommunications offers corporations.

A number of variables determine which headquarters concentrate in major international financial and business centers. First, how we measure or simply count headquarters makes a difference. Frequently, the key measure is the size of the firm in terms of employment and overall revenue. Using this measure, some of the largest firms in the world are still manufacturing firms, and many of these have their main headquarters in proximity to their major factory complex, which is unlikely to be in a large city because of space constraints. Such firms *are* likely, however, to have secondary headquarters for highly specialized functions in major cities. Furthermore, many manufacturing firms are oriented to the national

(Text continued on Page 82)

EXHIBIT 4.7a

The 25 Largest Nonfinancial Transnational Corporations, Ranked by Foreign Assets, 1990 (US$ billions and number of employees)

Rank	Corporation	Country	Industry[a]	Assets		Sales		Employment	
				Foreign	Total	Foreign	Total	Foreign	Total
1	Royal Dutch Shell	United Kingdom/Netherlands	Petroleum refining	69.2[b]	106.4	47.1[b]	106.5	99,000	137,000
2	Ford	United States	Motor vehicles and parts	55.2	173.7	47.3	97.7	188,904	370,383
3	GM	United States	Motor vehicles and parts	52.6	180.2	37.3	122	251,130	767,200
4	Exxon	United States	Petroleum refining	51.6	87.7	90.5	115.8	65,000	104,000
5	IBM	United States	Computers	45.7	87.6	41.9	69	167,868	373,816
6	British Petroleum	United Kingdom	Petroleum refining	31.6	59.3	43.3	59.3	87,200	118,050
7	Asea Brown Boveri	Switzerland	Industrial and farm equipment	26.9	30.2	25.6[d]	26.7	200,177	215,154
8	Nestlé	Switzerland	Food	—[c]	28	35.8	36.5	192,070	199,021
9	Philips Electronics	Netherlands	Electronics	23.3	30.6	28.8[d]	30.8	217,149	272,800
10	Mobil	United States	Petroleum refining	22.3	41.7	44.3	57.8	27,593	67,300
11	Unilever	United Kingdom/Netherlands	Food	—[c]	24.7	16.7[b]	39.6	261,000	304,000
12	Matsushita Electric	Japan	Electronics	—[c]	62	21	46.8	67,000	210,848
13	Fiat	Italy	Motor vehicles and parts	19.5	66.3	20.7[d]	47.5	66,712	303,238
14	Siemens	Germany	Electronics	—[c]	43.1	14.7[d]	39.2	143,000	373,000
15	Sony	Japan	Electronics	—[c]	32.6	12.7	20.9	62,100	112,900
16	Volkswagen	Germany	Motor vehicles and parts	—[c]	42	25.5[d]	42.1	95,934	268,744

17	Elf Aquitaine	France	Petroleum refining	17	42.6	11.4[d]	32.4	33,957	90,000
18	Mitsubishi	Japan	Trading	16.7	73.8	45.5	129.3	—	32,417
19	GE	United States	Electronics	16.5	153.9	8.3	57.7	62,580	298,000
20	Du Pont	United States	Chemicals	16	38.9	17.5	37.8	36,400	124,900
21	Alcatel Alsthom	France	Electronics	15.3	38.2	13	26.6	112,966	205,500
22	Mitsui	Japan	Trading	15	60.8	48.1	136.2	—	9,094
23	News Corporation	Australia	Publishing and printing	14.6	20.7	4.6	5.7	—	38,432
24	Bayer	Germany	Chemicals	14.2	25.4	20.3	25.9	80,000	171,000
25	B.A.T. Industries	United Kingdom	Tobacco	—[c]	48.1	16.5[d]	22.9	—	217,373

a. Industry classification of companies follows that in the Fortune Global 500 list in *Fortune*, July 29 1991 and the Fortune Global Service 500 list in *Fortune*, August 26 1991. In the Fortune classification, companies are included in the industry or service that represents the greatest volume of their sales; industry groups are based on categories established by the U.S. Office of Management and Budget. Several companies, however, are highly diversified.

b. Excludes other European countries.

c. Data for foreign assets not available; ranking is according to foreign assets estimated by the transnational corporations and management division on the basis of the ration of foreign to total employment, foreign to total fixed assets, or other similar ratios.

d. Includes export sales that are not separately reported.

Source: Based on UNCTAD, *Programme on Transnational Corporations*, company annual financial statements, WorldScope company accounts database, unpublished sources from companies, The Industrial Institute for Economic and Social Research (Stockholm, Sweden), and Stopford (1992). The WorldScope database uses standardized data definitions to adjust for differences in accounting terminology. Data for U.S. companies with fiscal year-end until January 15, 1991, are classified as 1990 data.

EXHIBIT 4.7b

The 25 Largest Nonfinancial Transnational Corporations Ranked by Foreign Assets, 1996 (US$ billions and number of employees)

Ranking by: Foreign Assets	Transnational Index[a]	Corporation	Country	Industry[b]	Assets Foreign	Assets Total	Sales Foreign	Sales Total	Employment Foreign	Employment Total
1	83	General Electric	United States	Electronics	82.8	272.4	21.1	79.2	84,000	239,000
2	32	Royal Dutch, Shell[c]	United Kingdom/ Netherlands	Petroleum expl./ref./dist.	82.1	124.1	71.1	128.3	79,000	101,000
3	75	Ford Motor Company	United States	Automotive	79.1	258	65.8	147	—[e]	371,702
4	22	Exxon Corporation	United States	Petroleum expl./ref./dist.	55.6	95.5	102	117	—[e]	79,000
5	85	General Motors	United States	Automotive	55.4	222.1	50	158	221,313	647,000
6	52	IBM	United States	Computers	21.4	81.1	46.6	75.9	121,655	240,615
7	79	Toyota	Japan	Automotive	39.2	113.4	51.7	109.3	34,837	150,736
8	49	Volkswagen Group	Germany	Automotive	—[d]	60.8	41	64.4	123,042	260,811
9	71	Mitsubishi Corporation	Japan	Diversified	—[d]	77.9	50.2	127.4	3,819	8,794
10	38	Mobil Corporation	United States	Petroleum expl./ref./dist.	31.3	46.4	53.1	80.4	22,900	43,000
11	3	Nestlé SA	Switzerland	Food	30.9	34	42	42.8	206,125	212,687
12	2	Asea Brown Boveri (ABB)	Switzerland/Sweden	Electrical equipment	—[d]	30.9	32.9	33.8	203,541	214,894
13	47	Elf Aquitaine SA	France	Petroleum expl./ref./dist.	29.3	47.5	26.6	44.8	41,600	85,400
14	14	Bayer AG	Germany	Chemicals	29.1	32	25.8	31.4	94,375	142,200
15	34	Hoechst AS	Germany	Chemicals	28	35.5	18.4	33.8	93,708	147,862
16	57	Nissan Motor Co., Ltd.	Japan	Automotive	27	58.1	29.2	53.8	—[e]	135,331
17	74	FIAT Spa	Italy	Automotive	26.9	70.6	19.8	51.3	90,390	237,865

18	8	Unilever	Netherlands/United Kingdom	Food	26.4	31	45	52.2	273,000	304,000
19	70	Daimler Benz AG	Germany	Automotive	—d	65.7	44.4	70.6	67,208	290,029
20	11	Philips Electronics N.V.	Netherlands	Electronics	24.5	31.7	38.9	40.9	21,600	262,500
21	9	Roche Holding AG	Switzerland	Pharmaceuticals	24.5	29.5	12.6	12.9	39,074	48,972
22	56	Siemens AG	Germany	Electronics	24.4	56.3	38.4	62.6	176,000	379,000
23	36	Alcatel Alsthom Cie	France	Electronics	23.5	48.4	24.6	31.6	112,820	190,600
24	40	Sony Corporation	Japan	Electronics	23.5	45.8	32.8	45.7	95,000	163,000
25	19	Total SA	France	Petroleum expl./ref./dist.	—d	30.3	25.8	34	—e	57,555

a. The index of transnationality is calculated as the average of three ratios: foreign assets to total assets, foreign sales to total sales, and foreign employment to total employment.

b. Industry classification for companies follows the U.S. Standard Industrial Classification as used by the U.S. Securities and Exchange Commission.

c. Foreign sales are outside Europe, whereas foreign employment is outside United Kingdom and the Netherlands.

d. Data on foreign assets are either suppressed to avoid disclosure or they are not available. In case of nonavailability, they are estimated on the basis of the ratio of foreign to total foreign to total assets or similar ratios.

e. Data on foreign employment are either suppressed to avoid disclosure or they are not available. In case of nonavailability, they are estimated on the basis of the ratio of foreign to total foreign to total assets or similar ratios.

f. Foreign assets, sales, and employment are outside of the United Kingdom and the Netherlands.

g. Foreign assets, sales, and employment are outside of the United Kingdom and Australia.

Source: UNCTAD/Erasmus University database, World Investment Report (1998:36-38).

EXHIBIT 4.8

Distribution of Outward Affiliates of Major Investing Countries by Sector, Various Years, 1980 to 1990 (number and percentage)

Country	Year		Sectors			
			All	Primary	Manufacturing	Services
Germany, Federal Republic of[a]	1984	Number	14,657	558	4,936	9,163
		Percentage	100	4	34	63
	1990	Number	19,352	422	5,729	13,201
		Percentage	100	2	30	68
Japan[b]	1980	Number	3,567	194	1,587	1,786
		Percentage	100	5	44	50
	1990	Number	7,986	194	3,408	4,384
		Percentage	100	2	43	55
United States[c]	1982	Number	18,339	995	7,005	10,339
		Percentage	100	5	38	56
	1989	Number	18,899	785	7,552	10,562
		Percentage	100	4	40	56

a. Includes only affiliates whose balance sheet total exceeds DM 500,000.

b. Includes only nonbank affiliates that responded to a questionnaire on foreign direct investment (FDI) and that continued their foreign operations.

c. Includes only affiliates whose assets, sales, or income exceeded $3 million.

Sources: UNCTC, The Determinants of Foreign Direct Investment (1992); Japan, Ministry of International Trade and Industry; United States Department of Commerce (1985, 1992).

EXHIBIT 4.9

Geographical Concentration of Transnational Corporations, by Foreign Assets, Foreign Sales, Foreign Employment, and Number of Entries, 1996 (percentage of total and number)

Region/Economy	Foreign Assets	Foreign Sales	Foreign Employment	Number of Entries
European Union	37	38	46	39
France	9	8	9	11
Germany	12	11	12	9
Netherlands	8	8	10	3
United Kingdom	12	12	15	11
Japan	16	26	10	18
United States	33	27	20	30
Total value (US$ billions and number)	1,475.0	2,147.9	4,447,732	100

Source: UNCTAD, World Investment Report (1997:35).

market and do not need to be located in a city's national business center. Thus, the much-publicized departure of major headquarters from New York City in the 1960s and 1970s involved these types of firms. If we look at the Fortune 500 list of the largest U.S. firms, we will see that many have left New York City and other large cities. If, however, instead of size we measure share of total firm revenue coming from international sales, a large number of firms that are not on the Fortune 500 list come into play. In the case of New York, for example, the results change dramatically: In 1990, 40% of U.S. firms with half their revenue from international sales have their headquarters in New York City.

Second, the nature of the urban system in a country is a factor in the geographic distribution of headquarters. Sharp urban primacy will tend to entail a disproportionate concentration of headquarters no matter what measure one uses. Third, different economic histories and business traditions may combine to produce different results.

Finally, headquarters concentration may be linked to a specific economic phase. For instance, unlike New York's loss of top *Fortune* 500 headquarters, Tokyo has gained these types of headquarters. Osaka and Nagoya, the two other major economic centers in Japan, lost headquarters to Tokyo. This change seems to be linked to the increasing internationalization of the Japanese economy and the corresponding increase in central command and servicing functions in Tokyo, Japan's major international business center. In the case of Japan, extensive government regulation over the economy is an added factor contributing to headquarters location in Tokyo because all international activities have to go through various government approvals.

In brief, understanding the meaning of headquarters concentration requires differentiation along the variables just described. Although headquarters are still disproportionately concentrated in major cities, the patterns becoming evident in the mid-1980s do represent a change.

The discussion about producer services, the producer services complex, and the locational patterns of headquarters point to two significant developments over the last 10 to 15 years. One is the growing service intensity in the organization of the economy, and the other, the emergence of a producer services complex that, although strongly geared toward the corporate sector, is far more likely to remain concentrated in urban centers than are the headquarters it serves.

The subject of the rise of the producer services complex inevitably brings up the financial and real estate crisis of the late 1980s and early 1990s, since so much of the highly speculative character of the 1980s was engineered by financial, legal, accounting, and other kindred experts in the major international business centers.

Impact of the Late 1980s Financial Crisis on Global City Functions: The Case of New York City

The high level of speculation and profitability that fed growth in the 1980s was clearly unsustainable. The late 1980s financial crisis raises two possibilities. One is that it represents a true crisis of an economic system; the other, that it is instead a sharp readjustment to more sustainable levels of speculation and profitability. New York was the first of the major international financial centers to experience massive losses. Its post-1987 evolution may provide some useful insights into the interaction between crisis and readjustment in the dominant sector.

Employment in banking in the city fell from 169,000 in 1989 to 157,000 in 1991. Most of this loss (more than 10,000 jobs) was in domestic banking. It should also be noted that some of these losses were the result of the massive restructuring within the industry, including mergers among large domestic banks.

In the securities industry, an area that suffered some of the sharpest job losses after the 1987 stock market crisis, New York City remains strong. Ten years later, New York City housed 11 of the world's 25 largest security firms and accounted for 79% of the combined assets of these firms. City firms and their overseas affiliates acted as advisers for almost 80% of the value of all international mergers and acquisitions at the height of the financial boom in the mid-1980s. They remained strong in the financial boom of the mid-1990s. Because the securities industry is almost completely export oriented, it may well be less sensitive to crises in the U.S. economy and in New York City specifically.

Even after the financial crisis of 1997-98, New York City continues to function as an important international center and continues to be dominated by financial and related industries. According to many analysts, the 1987 crisis was a much-needed adjustment to the excesses of the 1980s. The 1997-98 crisis had far less of an impact on New York City (and London) than did the 1987 crisis. Within the United States, New York City remains the banking capital of the country, leading in total assets, number of banks, and volume in various markets (currency, options trading, merchant banking). Worldwide, it is the leading financial center along with London.

Furthermore, foreign banking is a growth sector in New York City and may well be a key factor in the continuing role of the city as a leading financial center for the world. So even as Japanese and European banks were surpassing U.S. banks in size (see Exhibit 2.2), they had offices in New York City. Indeed, in 1990, New York City surpassed London in its number of international bank offices. By the end of the 1990s, London and New York City are the leading banking and financial centers in the world. Notwithstanding reductions in the domestic banking industry and major crises in several industry branches, New York remains truly a platform for international operations.

What emerges from these developments is that New York City may retain its central role as a financial center but with a far greater participation by foreign firms making loans, selling financial services, and assisting in mergers and acquisitions. The same is the case for London. The job losses and bankruptcies in the securities industry from 1987 pointed to the possibility of a major transformation in the role of Wall Street and other stock markets, most particularly in that large corporations can bypass stock markets to raise investment capital. But drastic change does not spell the end of Wall Street or the city of London. Furthermore, we now know that the actual change proved to be far less drastic and that by the early 1990s Wall Street was once again booming. The 1987 and subsequent crises may prove to be partly a restructuring process from which Wall Street emerged as a transformed market, but without losing an international base and continuing as a provider of the most specialized and complex services.

Conclusion: Cities as Postindustrial Production Sites

A central concern in this chapter was to look at cities as production sites for the leading service industries of our time and hence to recover the infrastructure of activities, firms, and jobs that is necessary to run the advanced corporate economy. Specialized services are usually understood in terms of specialized outputs rather than the production process involved. A focus on the production process allows us (1) to capture some of the locational characteristics of these service industries and (2) to examine the proposition that there is a producer services complex that, although catering to corporations, has distinct locational and production characteristics. It is this producer services complex more than headquarters of firms generally that benefits and often needs a city location. We see this dynamic for agglomeration operating at different levels of the urban hierarchy, from the global to the regional.

At the global level, a key dynamic explaining the place of major cities in the world economy is that they concentrate the infrastructure and the servicing that produce a capability for global control. The latter is essential if geographic dispersal of economic activity—whether factories, offices, or financial markets—is to take place under continued concentration of ownership and profit appropriation. This capability for global control cannot simply be subsumed under the structural aspects of the globalization of economic activity. It needs to be produced. It is insufficient to posit, or take for granted, the awesome power of large corporations.

By focusing on the production of this capability, we add a neglected dimension to the familiar issue of the power of large corporations. The emphasis shifts to the *practice* of global control: the work of producing and reproducing the organization and management of a global production system and a global marketplace for finance, both under conditions of economic concentration. Power is essential in the organization of the world economy, but so is production: the production of those inputs that constitute the capability for global control and the infrastructure of jobs involved in this production. This allows us to focus on cities and on the urban social order associated with these activities.

5

Issues and Case Studies
in the New Urban Economy

Several of the questions raised in the preceding chapter can be fruitfully addressed through a closer look at cases of individual cities and issues of the new urban economy. The organizing focus of this chapter is the growing concentration and specialization of financial and service functions that lie at the heart of the new urban economy at a time when we might expect the development of global telecommunications to be pushing them toward geographic dispersal. These specific case studies provide insights into the dynamics of contemporary globalization processes as they materialize in specific places. They also present, in somewhat schematic form, a logic of inquiry into these issues that can be replicated in studies of other cities. Finally, we have chosen for our three case studies cities that are not among the absolute top tier, such as Miami and Toronto, and are less known as sites for global processes.

We begin with an examination of the formation of global city functions. We have chosen Miami to illustrate this process because we can see there, in incipient form, the implantation of the growth dynamic described in Chapter 4. The question here is, Under what conditions do global city functions materialize? Our second case study is Toronto, a city that built up its financial district over only the last 15 years and hence could have opted for far more dispersal than can old financial centers. Focusing on a broader, national geography, we chose Sydney in Australia to examine how these tendencies toward concentration operate in the case of a multipolar urban system and a vast, rich economy. Can we expect a similar multipolarity in the distribution of financial functions? After looking at these cities as laboratory cases, we examine the general trend toward concentration in financial and top-level service functions against a broader historical and geographic perspective. Is this a new trend? Is it likely to remain unchanged? Finally, we examine the question of urban form: Have the new information technologies changed the spatial correlates of the center, the terrain where the international financial and business center and the producer services complex materialize?

The Development of Global City Functions: The Case of Miami

Each of today's global cities has a specific history that has contributed to its current status. Many of the world's major cities enjoyed a long history as banking and trading centers or as capitals of commercial empires.[1] This fact raises two immediate questions: What aspects of today's global cities are a continuation of past functions? How can global city functions emerge in cities that lack a long history as international banking and trading centers?

Miami is a case in point. On one hand, it is a city with a short history, one lacking any significant international functions. On the other hand, its large Cuban immigration led to the development in the 1960s and 1970s of an international trading complex oriented to Latin America and the Caribbean. The relative simplicity of Miami's history and of its international trading functions makes it relatively easy to disentangle two key processes: (1) the continuity of the Cuban-led trading complex and (2) the formation of a new business complex responding to the demands created by current processes of globalization. The case of Miami thus helps us understand how a city can become a site for global city functions.

A growing number of U.S., European, and Asian firms have set up offices in Miami since the late 1980s. Miami now has the fourth largest concentration of foreign bank offices in the United States, right behind New York, Los Angeles, and Chicago and ahead of San Francisco, Boston, or Atlanta. Eastman Kodak moved its headquarters for Latin American operations from Rochester in New York to Miami, and Hewlett-Packard made a similar move from Mexico City to Miami. Firms and banks from Germany, France, Italy, South Korea, Hong Kong, and Japan, to name but some, have all opened offices and brought in significant numbers of high-level personnel. Alongside these developments, there has been sharp growth in financial and specialized services for business. Miami's media image was so strongly associated with immigration and drugs that the formation of a new international corporate sector did not receive much attention until the mid-1990s.

---

1. For two extraordinary and different types of accounts, see Braudel (1984) and King (1990).

The scale of these developments leads us to ask whether Miami, although not quite a global city of the first rank, may have emerged as a site for global city functions. The case of Miami is also interesting because the city already has a concentration of international trading operations built and owned in good part by the prosperous resident Cuban elite (Portes and Stepick 1993). Since their arrival in the 1960s after the 1959 Castro revolution, the Cuban community has built an impressive international trading entrepôt, with a strong presence of firms and banks from Latin America and the Caribbean. Is the existence of the Cuban enclave, then, with its multiple trading operations for the Caribbean and Latin America, the base on which these new global city functions developed? Or is the latter a somewhat autonomous process that certainly may benefit from the concentration of trading operations in Miami but that responds to a different logic? Does it represent a type of development that would have taken place anyway in the southern Atlantic region, although perhaps not in Miami without the Cuban enclave? In brief, what is the relation between these two processes, one shaped by past events and the other by the current demands of economic globalization?

Some of the hypotheses in the research literature on global cities are of interest here, especially those that examine the spatial and organizational forms assumed by economic globalization today and the actual work of running transnational economic operations. Figures on the growth of Miami's foreign banks, foreign headquarters, prime office space market, installation of major telecommunications facilities, high-income residential and commercial gentrification, and high priced international tourism all point to developments that transcend both the Cuban enclave and the Caribbean import/export enterprises in its midst. They point to another dynamic, one at least partly rooted in the new forms of economic globalization. They suggest that the growth of the new international corporate sector in Miami is part of this new dynamic rather than a mere expansion of the Cuban enclave's Latin American and Caribbean trading operations.

As described in Chapter 2, overall international business transactions with Latin America are growing rapidly. Total foreign direct investment in the Latin American economies grew from an average of US$6.1 billion in 1984-87 to $28.7 billion in 1994, and nearly doubled to $56.1 billion in 1997. As we saw there, privatization, deregulation of stock markets and other financial markets, and the new export-oriented development model in most of Latin America are major factors. These are all extremely complicated transactions that require vast specialized inputs—a far cry from the earlier type of trading that initiated the growth of Miami in the 1970s.

One could argue that democratization and the opening of Latin American economies to foreign trade and investment should have made Miami less rather than more important. Yet Miami saw sharp growth in the concentration of top-level managerial and specialized servicing activities. And as we saw in Chapters 3 and 4, this is one type of evidence for cities that function as international business centers.

Over the last few years, Miami has also become a major administrative, managerial, and decision-making center. Since the mid-1980s, the city has received a significant inflow of secondary headquarters. Large U.S. firms are reorganizing and expanding their Miami offices to handle new trade with Latin America. For example, Texaco's Miami office increased its staff by 33% since 1987 to handle new operations in Colombia and Venezuela. And so did Miami's AT&T headquarters, which won 60% of a contract to upgrade Mexico's telecommunications infrastructure—no small job. Major companies such as France's Aerospatiale, Italy's Rimoldi, and Japan's Mitsui opened operations in Miami. At the same time, Miami is a key platform for the operations of Latin American firms in the United States and perhaps, eventually, even for operations with other Latin American countries. In addition, private investment in real estate, often for company housing by German, French, and Italian firms, has grown sharply in the 1990s. Miami now concentrates transnational-level functions that used to be located in a variety of other areas. For instance, GM relocated its headquarters for coordinating and managing Latin American operations from São Paulo in Brazil to Miami.

Miami also has significant international banking representation from Latin America, the Caribbean, Europe, and Asia. By 1992, Miami had 65 foreign bank offices. This is a small number compared with 464 in New York and 133 in Los Angeles at the time, but it was not far from Chicago's 80 and made Miami the fourth U.S. city in number of foreign bank offices. By 1998, Miami's number had grown to 77. This is not insignificant if we consider that the 10 top cities accounted for over 90% of all foreign bank offices in the United States, with New York City accounting for almost half. Almost all Miami offices were bank agencies and representative offices, both of which are full banking offices.[2]

Miami is becoming a major telecommunications center for the region, which will further concentrate command functions there. For instance, AT&T laid the first undersea fiber-optic cable to South America, connecting southern Florida to Puerto Rico, the Dominican Republic, Jamaica,

---

2. The count for foreign bank offices includes foreign bank agencies and representative offices, and so-called Edge-Act corporations.

and Colombia. The company worked with Italy, Spain, and Mexico to build another fiber-optic link between those countries, the Caribbean, and Florida. Finally, we cannot overlook the significant concentration of telecommunication facilities associated with the large regional CIA headquarters, which can be of benefit, often indirectly, to commercial operations (Grosfoguel 1993).

We can think of the Miami metropolitan area as a platform for international business transactions, a center for the long-distance coordination and management of transactions in Latin America and the Caribbean for firms from any part of the world interested in doing business in these regions.

The growing importance of these servicing and financing operations is reflected in the ascendance of these activities in the region's employment structure, the expansion of communications facilities, and the large supply of prime office space. It is not simply that employment in services grew by 46.3% from 1970 to 1990, partly as a function of population growth and general economic restructuring, but also that there has been a sharp recomposition in the components of services (Perez-Stable and Uriarte 1993). In the recent past, domestic tourism and retail had been the driving growth sectors; by the late 1980s, it was finance and producer services, as well as new types of tourism—mostly international and high priced—and new types of retail—mostly upscale and catering to the expanded national and foreign corporate sector.

The key to the newly emergent Miami-area economy lies in the growth of producer services industries. Employment in these sectors almost doubled from 1970 to 1989 in Dade County, the Miami metropolitan area, reaching 20% of all private sector employment. Employment in banking and in credit agencies almost tripled. Business services more than doubled; so did specialized services, from engineering to accounting. The sharpest increase was the quadrupling in legal services employment. (Although part of the latter may be a result of the growth of Miami's other major industries, drugs and guns, at least some of it is linked to the growth of international finance and service functions.) In the mid-1990s, employment in the leading sectors stabilized.

Industrial services are also a factor in these developments. Miami is a great transportation hub, with ports and airports that are among the busiest in the United States. The city's and its neighboring ports move more containerized cargo to Latin America than any other U.S. port. In terms of turnover of foreign passengers and cargo, Miami's airport is second only to New York City's Kennedy. In addition, the region now has a growing concentration of manufacturing firms aimed at the export market in the Caribbean and Latin America, as these areas become major buyers of U.S. goods. Miami's Free Trade Zone is one of the largest in the country.

All of this growth needs to be housed. By the end of the 1980s, Miami was in the top 15 U.S. metropolitan areas in terms of prime rental office space supply. Although Miami's 44 million square feet were a fraction of top-listed New York City's 456.6 million square feet at the time, it was not insignificant.

Why has this growth of a new international corporate sector taken place in Miami? Would these functions have been performed elsewhere had it not been for the Cuban enclave? The growth of the Cuban enclave supported the internationalization of the city by creating a pool of bilingual managers and entrepreneurs skilled in international business. This resource gave the city an edge in the competition for the Latin trade. But is it sufficient to explain the subsequent agglomeration of U.S., European, and Asian corporate headquarters and bank offices and the sharp expansion in financial services?

The development of global city functions in Miami is centered on the recent sharp growth in the absolute levels of international investment in Latin America, the growing complexity of the transactions involved, and the trend for firms all over the world to operate globally. The Cuban enclave represents a significant set of resources, from international servicing know-how to Spanish-speaking personnel. But the particular forms of economic globalization evident over the last decade have implanted a growth dynamic in Miami that is distinct from the enclave, although benefiting from it. At the same time, although the new international corporate sector has made Miami a site for the transnational operations of firms from all over the world, these operations are still largely confined to Latin America and the Caribbean. In that sense, we can think of Miami as a site for global city functions, although not a global city in the way that Paris or London is.

The Growing Density and Specialization of Functions in Financial Districts: Toronto

The leading financial districts in the world have all had rapid increases in the density of office buildings during the 1980s. There has also been a strong tendency toward growing specialization in the major activities housed in these buildings. It could be argued that one of the reasons for this continuing and growing concentration in a computer age is that these are mostly old districts that have inherited an infrastructure built in an earlier, pretelecommunications era and hence do not reflect a *necessary* form. In other words, the new density evident today would not be the result of agglomeration economies in the financial and corporate services complex but, rather, would be an imposed form from the past.

The case of Toronto is interesting because so much of the city's financial district was built in the mid- to late 1980s, and it entered that decade with a far smaller and less prominent financial district than cities such as New York, London, or Amsterdam (City of Toronto 1990; Todd 1993, 1995), while not having gained the ascendance over Montreal it now has (Levine 1990). Furthermore, massive construction of office buildings also took place in the wider region around the city, including installation of all the most advanced communications facilities the 1980s offered. In terms of building and telecommunications technology, this might seem to be a case in which much of the office infrastructure of the financial sector could have been located outside the small confines of the downtown. But that did not happen. According to Gunther Gad, a leading analyst of the spatial aspects of the office economy in Toronto, the demand was for a high-density office district"; 'long walks' of 15 minutes are resented" (Gad 1991:206-07; see also Canadian Urban Institute 1993).

Initially, Toronto's downtown office district housed manufacturing and wholesaling firms, the printing plants of the two main newspapers, and a large number of insurance firms. Much space was also allocated to retail; at one time, there were street level shops and eating places on most blocks. Those were put underground, further raising the actual and visual office density of the district. Until the 1950s, the present financial district was still the general office district of the metropolitan area, containing the headquarters of firms in all major industries. Beginning at that time and continuing into the subsequent two decades, firms in a broad range of industries—insurance, publishing, architecture, engineering—moved out.

This is a pattern evident in other major cities: London saw a large number of its insurance headquarters move out; the downtowns of Frankfurt and Zurich became increasingly specialized financial districts; and New York saw the development of a new midtown office district that accommodated growing industries such as advertising and legal services, leaving Wall Street to become an increasingly specialized financial district.

Between 1970 and 1989, office employment in Toronto's financial district doubled, and its share of all employment rose from 77.6% to 92.3%, with a corresponding fall in nonoffice jobs. But the composition of office jobs also changed from 1970 to 1989. Thus, the share of the insurance industry in all office activities fell from 14.6% to 9.8%, although it grew in absolute numbers. By 1989, well over half of all office employment was in finance, insurance, and real estate, and 28% in producer services. Gad (1991) found that banks, trust companies, investment services (including securities dealers), and real estate developers grew strongly in the 1980s. Other producer services also grew very strongly: legal services, accounting, management consulting, and computer services. But others, such as architectural and engineering consulting, did not. By the early 1990s, Toronto's financial markets ranked fourth overall in North America (Todd 1995). By 1997, Toronto's exchanges ranked seventh in the world, right below Zurich (see Exhibit 2.7 here).

A more detailed analysis shows yet other patterns. Until the 1970s, it was typical for a large bank in a major city of a developed country to consolidate all its operations in one building in a city's financial district. By the early 1980s, it had become common for such institutions to relocate back-office jobs and branch functions out of the main office in the financial district to other parts of a city's larger metropolitan region. The same pattern was evident in Toronto. Spatial dispersal of more routine operations also took place within other industries—again, a pattern fairly typical for all major business centers. These trends, together with the growth in the share of high-level professional and managerial jobs, have led to an employment structure in Toronto's financial district that is highly bimodal, with 41% of all workers in top-level jobs—up from 31.5% in 1980. Professional jobs grew by 24% from 1996-1998.

By the early 1990s, Toronto had the largest concentration of corporate offices in Canada. Fifty of Canada's largest financial institutions are headquartered in Toronto, with 39 of them in the financial district. They include the majority of Canada's banks, foreign banks, and trust companies. Many other financial institutions have Toronto head-office subsidiaries, and some insurance companies located elsewhere have investment departments in Toronto. Here also are Canada's largest investment firms, several of the largest pension funds, and the various trade associations involved with finance and banking (Todd 1995).

Generally, top-level functions, and the most complex and innovative activities, are carried out in the financial district of major cities. Routine operations can be moved outside these financial districts. The more risk-laden, speculative activities, such as securities trading, have increased their share of activity in financial districts. The financial district in Toronto is the place where large, complex loans can be put together; where complicated mergers and acquisitions can be executed; where large firms requiring massive investment capital for risky activities, such as real estate development or mining, can secure what they need, often combining several lenders and multiple lending strategies (Gad 1991).

This is the specialized production process that takes place in the financial districts of today's major cities. The nature of these activities—the large amounts of capital, the complexity, the risk, and the multiplicity of firms involved in each transaction—also contributes to the high density. On one hand, there is a built-in advantage in being located in a financial district where all the crucial players are located; on the other, the risk, complexity, and speculative character of much of this activity raises the importance of face-to-face interaction. The financial district offers multiple possibilities for face-to-face contact: breakfast meetings, lunches, inter- and intrafirm meetings, cocktail parties, and most recently, health clubs. These are all opportunities for regularly meeting with many of the crucial individuals, for developing trust (of a specific sort) with potential partners in joint offerings, and for making innovative proposals in terms of mergers and acquisitions or joint ventures. Telecommunications cannot replace these networks. The complexity, imperfect knowledge, high risk, and speculative character of many endeavors, as well as acceleration in the circulation of information and in the execution of transactions, heighten the importance of both personal contact and spatial concentration.

The case of Toronto suggests that the high density and specialization evident in all major financial districts is a response to the needs generated by current trends in the organization of the financial and related industries. Toronto could have built its financial sector on a more dispersed model, as did the headquarters of the major national and foreign firms that spread over its metropolitan area along hypermodern communications facilities. But it didn't, suggesting that the density of Toronto's downtown financial district is not the result of an inherited, old-fashioned built infrastructure, but a response to current economic requirements.

The Concentration of Functions and Geographic Scale: Sydney

The analysis of Toronto revealed two forms of concentration: One, the main focus of the section, was the disproportionate concentration of financial functions in one small district in the city. The other was the disproportionate concentration of all national financial and headquarter functions in Canada in a single city, Toronto. Are the tendencies toward concentration found in Toronto at the geographic scale of the country, unusual—particularly for countries continental in scale and characterized historically by multiple-growth poles all oriented toward the world markets?

Here we want to examine in some detail this second tendency, toward concentration at the national scale in continent-sized countries, by focusing on Australia. Along with Canada and the United States, Australia has an urban system characterized by considerable multipolarity. This effect has been strengthened in Australia by the fact that it is an island-continent, which has promoted a strong outward orientation in each of its major cities. We might expect, accordingly, to find at work strong tendencies toward the emergence of several highly internationalized financial and business centers. Or conversely, will we also see in Australia a space economy characterized by a disproportionate concentration of international business and financial functions in one city?

During the period from World War II to the 1970s, Australia became a very rich country with many large urban centers, thriving agricultural and manufacturing exports, and low unemployment. In the post-World War II period, Australia boasted several major urban areas and many growth poles. Melbourne, the old capital of the state of Victoria, had been and remained the traditional focus for commerce, banking, and headquarters and, generally, the place of old wealth in Australia.

As did other developed economies, Australia experienced considerable restructuring beginning in the early 1970s: declines in manufacturing employment, growth in service employment, a shift to information-intensive industries, and a growing internationalization of production processes, services, and investment. In the mid-1980s, financial institutions were deregulated and integrated into global financial markets. There were massive increases in foreign direct investment, with a shift from agriculture, mining, and manufacturing to real estate and services and from European to Asian sources. Asian countries are now the main source of foreign investment in all major industries, and there generally is a greater orientation of trading and investment toward the Pacific Rim (Daly and Stimson 1992). Producer services emerged as the major growth sectors throughout all the metropolitan areas and (combined with wholesale and retail and community services) accounted for 48% of all employment nationwide in Australia by the end of the 1980s. The fastest-growing export sectors were producer services and tourism.

The shift in investment in the 1980s from manufacturing to finance, real estate, and services became particularly evident in metropolitan areas (Stimson 1993). In this conjunction, Sydney emerges as the major destination of investment in real estate and finance. In 1982-83, investment in manufacturing in Sydney was A$1.15 billion compared with A$1.32 billion in finance, real estate, and business services. By 1984-85, these levels of investment had changed, respectively, to A$0.82 billion and A$1.49 billion. At lower levels, these trends were evident in other major urban areas (Stimson 1993:5). By 1986, however, there was a disproportionate concentration of finance and business services in Sydney that increasingly outdistanced other major cities. A massive real estate boom from 1985 to 1988 left Sydney the dominant market in Australia, both in levels of investment and in prime office space.

Sydney became Australia's main international gateway city and its only "world city," according to Daly and Stimson (1992; see also Brotchie et al. 1995). It has the largest concentration of international business and financial firms in Australia, having surpassed Melbourne, once the main economic capital of the country (see Exhibit 5.1). By 1990, about 150 international firms were headquartered in Sydney, compared with 43 in Melbourne. These represent 29 countries, including 48 firms from Japan, 29 from the United States, and 14 from the United Kingdom. Sydney had 10 commercial bank headquarters compared with 4 in Melbourne, and 81 in merchant banking compared with 6 in Melbourne. Sixty of Australia's largest 100 companies were headquartered in Sydney in 1989 compared with 45 in 1984; Melbourne had 29 in 1989 compared with 41 in 1984. By 1990, Sydney's stock market ranked 10th in the world, a position it still held in 1997 (see Exhibit 2.7 here). Australia is emerging as an attractive location for secondary headquarters of Asian firms, and Sydney, where the majority of international contacts can be made, is by far the preferred city (O'Connor 1990).

In its earlier phase, Australia had been dependent on foreign investment to develop its manufacturing, mining, and agricultural sectors. But the share and order of magnitude of foreign investment in the 1980s point to a qualitative transformation and, in that sense, to a process of economic internationalization. From 1983-84 to 1988-89, foreign direct investment in Australia grew at an average of 34% a year, from A$81.9 billion to A$222.9 billion. Foreign investment in manufacturing also grew at a high rate, at 29% per year; but it grew at 83% a year in finance, real estate, and business services. This investment increasingly came from Japan and Asia, with declining shares coming from the United States and the United Kingdom (which were the two major investors in the past). Japan's share rose by 280%, reaching almost 15% of all foreign direct investment by 1989. Since 1990, Singapore, Hong Kong, and Taiwan have also become significant investors. In the second half of the 1980s, particularly following the deregu-

EXHIBIT 5.1

Headquarters Concentration in Sydney and Melbourne, 1989

	Commercial Banks	Merchant Banks	International Firms	Top 100 Australian Corporations
Sydney	10	81	150	60 (45)[a]
Melbourne	4	6	43	29 (41)[a]

a. Figures in parentheses are for 1984.

Source: Based on data from Stimson, "Process of Globalisation and Economic Restructuring and the Emergence of a New Space Economy of Cities and Regions in Australia." (1993).

lation of financial institutions, trading enterprises and banks were the major conduits through which capital entered the country. The real estate boom was directly linked to foreign investment, as was the real estate crisis of 1989-90, when foreign investors ceased pouring money into these markets. Over 28% of all foreign direct investment in 1985-86 went into real estate, growing to 46% by 1988-89. Japanese investors accounted for over a third of this investment. In that same period, 70% of investment proposals in tourism were Japanese. Investments to develop tourism rose from $A400 million in 1982 to A$1.61 billion in 1989; from 1987 to 1990, the value of major tourism projects either under construction or committed more than doubled to A$23 billion. This foreign investment was increasingly and disproportionately concentrated in New South Wales, which accounted for a third of all such investment, and in Queensland, with 21%; this represents a shift away from older regions such as Melbourne and its state of Victoria. Almost half of all investments in New South Wales, which has Sydney as its capital, were in commercial real estate.

The geography of these investments is made even more specific if we consider that the bulk of them were in the central business districts (CBDs) of major cities, with Sydney the leading recipient. Between 1975 and 1984, foreign investors had financed about 10% of total investment in commercial real estate; between 1980 and 1984, there were actually declines, reflecting the fall in global foreign investment in the early 1980s. But they picked up shortly after that, and by 1984, about 15% of CBD offices in Sydney were foreign owned, compared with about 12.5% in Melbourne (Adrian 1984). In the second half of the 1980s, there were sharp increases in investments in all CBDs of major cities but especially in Sydney, Melbourne, and Brisbane. Stimson (1993) notes that by 1990, the value of land held by Japanese investors in Sydney's CBD was estimated at A$1.55 billion, all of which had been invested in the second half of the 1980s. At the height of the boom in 1988-89, the officially estimated value of land in Sydney's CBD was put at $17.4 billion, a 10th of which was owned by Japanese investors.[3] Melbourne's CBD was also the object of much foreign investment acquisition, with record levels of construction in commercial real estate. In Brisbane, over 40% of the total office floor space was built between 1983 and 1990. Since those boom years, levels of foreign investment have fallen equally sharply, leaving a depressed office market in CBDs, a situation evident in major business centers all over the world.

It would seem, then, that even at the geographic scale and economic magnitude of a country like Australia, the ascendance of finance and services along with internationalization contribute to the marked concentration of strategic functions and investment in one city. Several experts on the Australian economy have noted that its increasing internationalization and the formation of new linkages connecting regions, sectors, and cities to the global economy have been central elements in the economic restructuring of that country (Daly and Stimson 1992; O'Connor 1990; Rimmer 1988; Stimson 1993). This process happened with great rapidity when we consider that not until 1983-84 did Australia deregulate its financial system, opening it up to world competition. Foreign investment patterns, international air passenger travel and tourism, and the location of activities and headquarters dependent on global networks all reflect this process of internationalization and concentration.

Globalization and Concentration: The Case of Leading Financial Centers

All the major economies in the developed world display a similar pattern of sharp concentration of financial activity and related producer services in one center: Paris in France, Milan in Italy, Zurich in Switzerland, Frankfurt in Germany, Toronto in Canada, Tokyo in Japan, Amsterdam in the Netherlands, and, as we have just seen, Sydney in Australia. The evidence also shows that the concentration of financial activity in such leading cen-

---

3. Japanese purchases of real estate grew sharply in the late 1980s. As recently as 1986, the value of such purchases stood at A$119.5 million; by 1990, the value had risen to A$324 billion. The total value of Japanese acquisitions of real estate stood at A$2.696 trillion by July 1990, already reflecting some devaluation due to the crisis beginning in 1989-90. The burst of the so-called bubble economy in 1991 and the subsequent long-term economic crisis that continues today have brought these prices down drastically.

ters has actually increased over the last decade. Thus Basel, formerly a very important financial center in Switzerland, has now been completely overshadowed by Zurich (Keil and Ronneberger 1993); and Montreal, certainly the other major center in Canada two decades ago, has now been overtaken by Toronto (Levine 1990). Similarly, Osaka was once a far more powerful competitor with Tokyo in the financial markets in Japan than it had become by the late 1980s (Sassen 1991:chaps. 6, 7).

Is this tendency toward concentration within each country a new development for financial centers? A broader historical view points to some interesting patterns. Since their earliest beginnings, financial functions were characterized by high levels of concentration. They often operated in the context of empires, such as the British or Dutch empires, or quasi-empires, such as the disproportionate economic and military power of the United States in the world over the last 50 years.

The first financial centers were medieval Italian cities such as Florence, a city with one of the most stable currencies in Europe, the florin. By the 17th century, Amsterdam had taken over from these cities; it introduced central banking and the stock market, probably reflecting its vast international merchant and trading operations and Amsterdam's role as an unrivaled international center for trading and exchange. One hundred years later, London had emerged as the major international financial center and the major market for European government debt. London became the financial capital of the world clearly as a function of the British Empire. By 1914, New York, which had won its competition with Philadelphia and Boston for the banking business in the United States, emerged as a challenger to London. London, however, was also the strategic cog in the international financial system, a role that New York was not quite ready to assume. But after World War II, the immense economic might of the United States and the destruction of England and other European countries left New York the world's financial center.

Against this pattern of empires, the formation of nation-states represents a condition making possible a multiplicity of financial centers, typically the national capital in each country. Furthermore, the ascendance of mass manufacturing contributed to vast, typically regionally based fortunes and the formation of financial centers in those regions: Chicago and Osaka are only two examples. The renewed ascendance of finance in the 1980s, as we have seen, once again sharpened the tendencies toward concentration in a limited number of financial centers.

It would seem, then, that current developments are a continuation of an old pattern. We can begin to understand why, after a decade of massive growth in the absolute levels of financial activity worldwide, a handful of cities—New York, London, Tokyo, Paris, Frankfurt—should account for such a disproportionate share of all activity. For example, international bank lending grew from US$1.89 trillion in 1980 to US$6.24 trillion in 1991—a threefold increase in a decade—and to US$9.03 trillion in 1998 (see Exhibit 5.2). The same seven countries accounted for almost two-thirds of this lending in 1980 and saw their share rise to three-fourths in 1998, according to data from the Bank for International Settlements, the leading institution worldwide in charge of overseeing banking activity. There were compositional changes: Japan's share rose from 6.2% in 1980 to 15.1% in 1991 and to 19.8% in 1998. The United Kingdom's fell from 26.2% to 16.3% and 6.1% in 1998; the U.S. share hovered around 10%. All increased in absolute terms. Much of this lending activity was executed in the leading financial center of each of these countries, or in specialized markets, such as Chicago, which dominates the world's trading in futures, accounting for about 30% of worldwide contracts in options and futures by the late 1990s. Strong patterns of concentration are also evident in stock market capitalization and in foreign exchange markets (see Exhibit 5.3).

We should note again that this unchanged level of concentration is in the context of enormous absolute increases, deregulation, and globalization of the industry worldwide, which means that a growing number of countries have become integrated into the world markets. Furthermore, this unchanged level of concentration has happened at a time when financial services are more mobile than ever before: globalization, deregulation (an essential ingredient for globalization), and securitization have been the keys to this mobility, in the context of massive advances in telecommunications and electronic networks.[4] One result is growing competition among centers for hypermobile financial activity. In my view, there has been an overemphasis on competition in both general and specialized accounts on this subject. As Chapter 3 argued, there is also a functional division of labor among various major financial centers. In that single sense, we should also see at work here one system located in multiple countries.

The hypermobility of financial capital puts added emphasis on the importance of technology. It is now possible to move money from one part of the world to another and make deals without ever leaving the computer terminal. Thanks to electronics, there are now disembodied marketplaces—what we can think of as the cyberspace of international finance

---

4. Securitization is the replacement of traditional bank finance by tradable debt; for example, a mortgage is bundled up along with thousands of others into a package that can be traded on specialized markets. This is one of the major innovations in the financial industry in the 1980s. Securitization made it possible to sell all kinds of (supposedly worthy) debt, thereby adding to the overall volume of transactions in the industry.

EXHIBIT 5.2

International Bank Lending, by Country, Selected Years, 1980 to 1998 (percentage, US$ trillions)

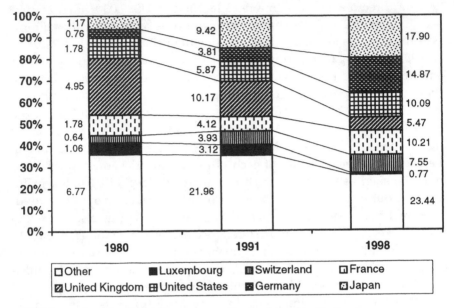

| Other | Luxembourg | Switzerland | France |
| United Kingdom | United States | Germany | Japan |

a. 1980 figures based on West German reporting banks and institutions.

Source: Based on data from the Bank for International Settlements, 62nd and 69th Annual Reports (1992, 1999).

(Sassen 1998:chap. 9). NASDAQ (National Association of Securities Dealers Automated Quotations) and the foreign exchange markets, unlike the regular stock market with its trading floor, are examples of disembodied markets.

Yet the trend toward concentration still continues unabated—indeed, with renewed vigor. Furthermore, much of the discussion around the formation of a single European market and financial system has raised the possibility, and even the need, for a European financial system made competitive by centralizing financial functions and capital in a limited number of cities, rather than maintaining the current structure in which each country has a financial center.

These tendencies toward concentration seem to be built into the nature of such financial centers. Centers at the top are characterized by a multiplicity of financial institutions and markets and significant shares of world activity in various markets. They usually have a large number of

EXHIBIT 5.3

Foreign Exchange Turnover, by Country (Daily Averages), 1989 and 1998 (US$ billions)

	1989	*1998*
United Kingdom	184.0	637.3
United States	115.2	350.9
Japan	110.8	148.6
Switzerland	56.0	81.7
Singapore	55.0	139.0
Hong Kong	48.8	78.6
Australia	28.9	46.6
France	23.2	71.9
Total "net-gross" turnover	717.9	1971.0

Source: Based on data from the Bank for International Settlements, *Central Bank Survey April 1998* (1999).

banks and other institutions that account for a significant share of international lending, foreign exchange trading, and fund management. They also have large or significant markets in tradable securities—whether bonds, stocks, or their derivatives.

Among the large financial centers, some are dominated by international business and others by domestic business. Thus, London, with its strong Eurodollar markets and foreign exchange markets, is extremely international, whereas New York and Tokyo, with their enormous national economies, inevitably are going to have a very large incidence of domestic borrowers, lenders, and investors. The sharpest competition among the international financial centers is in the capital markets; some of the capital markets are extremely international, notably the foreign exchange and the Eurodollar markets. London has a very large share of these markets. Finally, the globalization of the industry has raised the level of complexity of transactions, and deregulation has promoted the invention of many new, complex instruments. This change clearly has raised the importance of the leading centers insofar as they are the only ones with the capability to handle such levels of complexity.

In the next section, we examine these issues in greater detail with a particular focus on the networks that connect these centers and the impact of digitalization on the question of place.

Why Do We Need Financial Centers in the Global Digital Era?

The global financial system has reached levels of complexity that require the existence of a cross-border network of financial centers to service the operations of global capital. But this network of financial centers will increasingly differ from earlier versions of the "international financial system." In a world of largely closed national financial systems, each country duplicated most of the necessary functions for its economy; collaborations among different national financial markets were often no more than the execution of a given set of operations in each of the countries involved, as in clearing and settlement. With few exceptions, such as the offshore markets and some of the large banks, the international system consisted of a string of closed domestic systems.

The global integration of markets pushes toward the elimination of various redundant systems and makes collaboration a far more complex matter, one that has the perhaps ironic effect of raising the importance of leading financial centers. Rather than each country with its own center for global operations, we are likely to see a leaner system, with fewer strategic centers and more hierarchy. In this context, London and New York with their enormous concentrations of resources and talent will continue to be powerhouses in the global network for the most strategic and complex operations for the system as a whole. They are the leading exporters of financial services and typically part of any major international public offering, whether it is the privatization of British Telecom or of France Telecom. But the formation of a single-currency Eurozone will spell the end of an era in which each country had its full-fledged financial center. Very likely is a steep hierarchy with Frankfurt at the top in the Eurozone and a crisscross of alliances between Frankfurt and the other major centers and between the other centers without Frankfurt.

The "international financial centers" of many countries around the world will increasingly fulfill gateway functions for the "in and out" circulation of national and foreign capital. The incorporation of a growing number of these financial centers is one form through which the global financial system expands: Each of these centers is the nexus between that country's wealth and the global market and between foreign investors and that country's investment opportunities. The overall sources and destinations of investment therewith grow in number. Gateway functions will be their main mechanism for integration into the global financial market rather than, say, the production of innovations to package the capital flowing in and out. The complex operations will be executed by the top investment, accounting, and legal services firms, through affiliates, branches, direct imports of those services, or some other form of transfer.

These gateways for the global market are also gateways for the dynamics of financial crises: Capital can flow out as easily and quickly as it flows in. And what was once thought of as "national" capital can now as easily join the exodus: For instance, during the Mexico crisis of December 1994, we now know that the first capitals to flee the Mexican markets were national, not foreign, and in the flight out of Brazil of an estimated US$1 billion a day by early September 1998, not all of it was foreign.

Because the globally integrated financial system is not only about competition between countries, we will see an increase in specialized collaborative efforts between these centers. Nobody would really gain from crushing Tokyo or Hong Kong. The ongoing growth of London, New York, or Frankfurt is in part a function of a global network of financial centers.

Finally, while electronic networks will grow in number and in scope, they will not eliminate the need for financial centers. Rather, they will intensify the networks connecting such centers in strategic or functional alliances, most dramatically illustrated by the new linkup, announced in July 1998, between the exchanges of Frankfurt and London. Such alliances may well evolve into the equivalent of the cross-border mergers and acquisitions of firms. Electronic trading will also contribute a radically new pattern whereby one market—for instance, Frankfurt's Deutsche Eurex—can operate on screens in many other markets around the world or whereby one brokerage firm, Cantor Fitzgerald, can (as of September 1998) have its prices of Treasury futures listed on screens used by traders all around the United States.

But electronic trading will not eliminate the need for financial centers because these combine multiple resources and talents necessary for executing complex operations and servicing global firms and markets. Frankfurt's electronic futures network is actually embedded in a network of financial centers. And broker Cantor Fitzgerald has an alliance with the Board of Trade of New York to handle its computerized sale of Treasury futures. Financial centers cannot be reduced to their exchanges. They are part of a far more complex architecture, and they constitute far more complex structures within that architecture.

In the Digital Era: More
Concentration than Dispersal

What really stands out in the evidence for the global financial industry is the extent to which there is a sharp concentration of the shares of many financial markets in a few financial centers. This trend toward consolidation in a few centers is also evident within countries. In the United States for instance, New York concentrates all the leading investment banks with only one other major international financial center in this enormous country, Chicago. Sydney and Toronto have equally gained power in continental-sized countries and have taken over functions and market share from what were once the major commercial centers—respectively, Melbourne and Montreal. So have São Paulo and Bombay, which gained share and functions from, respectively, Rio de Janeiro in Brazil and New Delhi and Calcutta in India. These are all enormous countries, and one might have thought that they could sustain multiple major financial centers. In France, Paris today concentrates larger shares of most financial sectors than it did 10 years ago, and once-important stock markets such as Lyon have become "provincial," even though Lyon is today the hub of a thriving economic region. Milan privatized its exchange in September 1997 and electronically merged Italy's 10 regional markets. Frankfurt now concentrates a larger share of the financial market in Germany than it did in the early 1980s, and so does Zurich, which once had Basel as a very significant competitor of sorts. For instance, by 1997 Frankfurt's market capitalization was five times greater than all other regional markets in Germany combined, whereas in 1992, it was only twice as large. This story can be repeated for many countries. What stands out is that this pattern toward the consolidation of one leading financial center is a function of rapid growth in the sector, not of decay in the losing cities.

We are seeing, then, both consolidation in fewer major centers across and within countries *and* a sharp growth in the numbers of centers that become part of the global network as countries deregulate their economies. São Paulo and Bombay, for instance, joined the global financial network so to speak after Brazil and India deregulated, at least partly, their financial systems. This mode of incorporation into the global network is often at the cost of losing functions that they had when they were largely national centers, as the leading financial, accounting, and legal services firms enter their markets to handle the new cross-border operations. The incorporation typically happens without a gain in the share of the global market that they can command even though they add to the total volume in the global market.

Why is it that at a time of rapid growth in the network of financial centers, in overall volumes, and in electronic networks, we have such high concentration of market shares in the leading centers? Both globalization and electronic trading are about expansion and dispersal beyond what had been the confined realm of national economies and floor trading. Indeed, given globalization and electronic trading one might well ask why financial centers matter at all.

Agglomeration in the Digital Era?

The continuing weight of major centers is, in a way, countersensical, as is, for that matter, the existence of an expanding network of financial centers. The rapid development of electronic exchanges, the growing digitalization of much financial activity, the fact that finance has become one of the leading sectors in a growing number of countries, and that it is a sector that produces a dematerialized, hypermobile product, all suggest that location should not matter. In fact, geographic dispersal would seem to be a good option given the high cost of operating in major financial centers, and differentiation would seem to eliminate most reasons for having a geographic base. Furthermore, the last 10 years have seen an increased geographic mobility of financial experts and financial services firms.

There has been geographic decentralization of certain types of financial activities, aimed at securing business in the growing number of countries becoming integrated into the global economy. Many of the leading investment banks have operations in more countries than they had 20 years ago. The same can be said for the leading accounting and legal services and other specialized corporate services. And it can be said for some markets: For example, in the 1980s, all basic wholesale foreign exchange operations were in London. Today, these are distributed among London and several other centers (even though their number is far smaller than the number of countries whose currency is being traded).

There are, in my view, at least three reasons that explain the trend toward consolidation in a few centers rather than massive dispersal. I developed this analysis in *The Global City* (Sassen 1991), focusing on New York, London, and Tokyo, and since then, events have made this even clearer and more pronounced.

1. *Social Connectivity.* First, while the new telecommunications technologies do indeed facilitate geographic dispersal of economic activities without losing system integration, they have also had the effect of strengthening the importance of central coordination and control functions for firms and, even, markets. (Let's remember that many financial markets have "owners," are run by firms so to speak, and hence also contain central management functions of sorts.) Indeed, for firms in any sector, operating a widely dispersed network of branches and affiliates and operating in multiple markets has made central functions far more com-

plicated. Their execution requires access to top talent, not only inside headquarters but also, more generally, to innovative milieus—in technology, accounting, legal services, economic forecasting, and all sorts of other, many new, specialized corporate services. Major centers have massive concentrations of state-of-the-art resources that allow them to maximize the benefits of telecommunications and to govern the new conditions for operating globally. Even electronic markets such as NASDAQ and E*Trade rely on traders and banks located somewhere, with at least some in a major financial center.

One fact that has become increasingly evident is that to maximize the benefits of the new information technologies, you need not only the infrastructure but a complex mix of other resources. Most of the value-added that these technologies can produce for advanced service firms lies in the externalities. And this means the material and human resources—state-of-the-art office buildings, top talent, and the social networking infrastructure that maximizes connectivity. Any town can have the fiber optic cables. But do they have the rest?

A second fact emerging with greater clarity concerns the meaning of "information." There are, one could say, two types of information. One is the datum: At what level did Wall Street close? Did Argentina complete the public sector sale of its water utility? Has Japan declared such and such bank insolvent? But there is a far more difficult type of "information," akin to an interpretation/evaluation/judgment. It entails negotiating a series of data and a series of interpretations of a mix of data in the hope of producing a higher-order datum. Access to the first kind of information is now global and immediate thanks to the digital revolution. You can be a broker in the Colorado mountains and have access to this type of information. But the second type of information requires a complicated mixture of elements—the social infrastructure for global connectivity—that gives major financial centers a leading edge.

You can, in principle, reproduce the technical infrastructure anywhere. Singapore, for example, has technical connectivity matching Hong Kong's. But does it have Hong Kong's social connectivity? When the more complex forms of information needed to execute major international deals cannot be gotten from existing databases, no matter what one can pay, then one needs the social information loop and the associated de facto interpretations and inferences that come with bouncing off information among talented, informed people. The importance of this input has given a whole new weight to credit rating agencies, for instance. Part of the rating has to do with interpreting and inferring. When this interpreting becomes "authoritative," it becomes "information" available to all. The process of making inferences/interpretations into information takes quite a mix of talents and resources.

Risk management, for example, which has become increasingly important with globalization due to the growing complexity and uncertainty that comes with operating in multiple countries and markets, requires enormous fine-tuning of central operations. We now know that many, if not most, major trading losses over the last decade have involved human error or fraud. The quality of risk management will depend heavily on the top people in a firm rather than simply on technical conditions, such as electronic surveillance. Consolidating risk management operations in one site, usually a central one for the firm, is now seen generally as more effective. We have seen this in the case of several major banks: Chase and Morgan Stanley Dean Witter in the United States, Deutsche Bank and Credit Suisse in Europe.

In brief, financial centers provide the social connectivity that allows a firm or market to maximize the benefits of its technological connectivity.

2. *Need for Enormous Resources.* Global players in the financial industry need enormous resources, a trend that is leading to rapid mergers and acquisitions of firms and strategic alliances between markets in different countries. These are happening on a scale and in combinations few would have foreseen just a few years ago. In 1999 alone, we saw a whole new wave of mergers, notably Citibank with Travellers Group (which few would have predicted just two years earlier), Salomon Brothers with Smith Barney, Bankers Trust with Alex Brown, and so on. This wave has been so sharp that now that firms such as Deutsche Bank and Dresdner Bank want to purchase a U.S. security firm, they complain of a lack of suitable candidates. Many analysts now think that midsize firms will find it difficult to survive in the global market, when there are global megafirms such as Merrill Lynch, Morgan Stanley Dean Witter, and Goldman, Sachs. We are also seeing mergers between accounting firms, law firms, insurance brokers—in brief, firms that need to provide a global service. Analysts foresee a system dominated by a few global investment banks and about 25 big fund managers. A similar scenario is also predicted for the global telecommunications industry, which will have to consolidate to offer a state-of-the-art, globe-spanning service to its global clients, among which are the financial firms.

Another kind of "merger" is the consolidation of electronic networks that connect a very select number of markets. One of Chicago's futures exchanges, the Board of Trade (BOT) is loosely linked to Frankfurt's futures exchange and the other to Paris's futures exchange (MATIF). The New

York Stock Exchange is considering linking up with exchanges in Canada and Latin America and has opened talks with the Paris Bourse. NASDAQ's parent is having similar talks with Frankfurt and London. Perhaps most spectacular was the announcement in July 1998 of a linkup between the London Stock Exchange and Frankfurt's Deutsche Borse; the goal is to attract the top 300 shares from all over Europe—a blue-chip European exchange. Paris reacted by proposing that some of the other major European exchanges should create an alternative alliance.

Will all of this mean the consolidation of a stratum of select financial centers at the top of the worldwide network of 30 or 40 cities through which the global financial industry operates? Yes. We now also know that a major financial center needs to have a significant share of global operations to be such. If Tokyo does not succeed in getting more of such operations, it is going to lose standing in the global hierarchy notwithstanding its importance as a capital exporter. This same capacity for global operations will keep New York at the top levels of the hierarchy, even though it is largely fed by the resources and the demand of domestic (though state-of-the-art) investors. And it will keep Chicago as a key player, notwithstanding the loss of some of its futures contracts.

Does the fact of fewer global players affect the spread of such operations? In my reading, not necessarily, but it will strengthen the hierarchy in the global network. For instance, institutional money managers around the world controlled approximately $15 trillion by early 1999. The worldwide distribution of equities under institutional management shows considerable spread among a large number of cities that have become integrated in the global equity market with deregulation of their economies and the whole notion of "emerging markets" as an attractive investment destination over the last few years. Thomas Financial (1999), for instance, has estimated that at the end of 1998, 25 cities accounted for 83% of the world's valuation. These 25 cities also account for roughly 48% of the total market capitalization of the world, which stood at US$22 trillion at the end of 1998. On the other hand, this global market is characterized by a disproportionate concentration in the top 6 or 7 cities. London, New York, and Tokyo together account for a third of the world's total equities under institutional management at the end of 1998. London and New York together account for well over half of the global currency exchange market.

These developments make clear a second important trend that in many ways specifies the current global era. These various centers don't just compete with each other: There is collaboration and division of labor. In the international system of the postwar decades, each country's financial center, in principle, covered the universe of necessary functions to service its national companies and markets. The world of finance was, of course, much simpler than it is today. In the initial stages of deregulation in the 1980s, there was a strong tendency to see the relations between the major centers as one of straight competition between New York, London, and Tokyo, the heavyweights in the system. But it was already clear then that there was a division of labor. What we are seeing now is yet a third pattern: strategic alliances not only between firms across borders but also between markets. There is competition, strategic collaboration, and hierarchy.

In brief, the need for enormous resources to handle increasingly global operations in combination with the growth of central functions described under Reason 1 produces strong tendencies toward concentration and hence hierarchy in an expanding network.

3. Denationalization of the Corporate Elite. Finally, national attachments and identities are becoming weaker for these global players and their customers. Thus, the major U.S. and European investment banks have set up specialized offices in London to handle various aspects of their global business. Even French banks have set up some of their global specialized operations in London, inconceivable even a few years ago and still not avowed in national rhetoric.

Deregulation and privatization have further weakened the need for *national* financial centers. The nationality question simply plays differently in these sectors than it did even a decade ago. Global financial products are accessible in national markets, and national investors can operate in global markets. It is interesting to see that investment banks used to split up their analysts team by country to cover a national market; now they are more likely to do it by industrial sector.

In my *Losing Control?* (Sassen 1996), I have described this process as the incipient denationalization of certain institutional arenas. I think such denationalization is a necessary condition for economic globalization as we know it today. The sophistication of this system lies in the fact that it needs only to involve strategic institutional areas—most national systems can be left basically unaltered. China is a good example. It adopted international accounting rules in 1993, necessary to engage in international transactions. But it did not have to go through a fundamental reorganization to do this. Japanese firms operating overseas adopted such standards long before Japan's government considered requiring them. In this regard, the wholesale side of globalization is quite different from the global mass consumer markets, in which success necessitates altering national tastes at a mass level. This process of denationalization will be facilitated by the current acquisitions of firms and property in all the Asian countries in crisis. In some ways, one might say that the Asian financial crisis has functioned as a mechanism to denationalize, at least partly, control over key sectors of economies that, while allowing the massive entry of foreign investment, never relinquished that control.

Major international business centers produce what we could think of as a new subculture. In a witty insight, *The Economist* titled one of its stories on the January 1997 World Economic Forum meeting held in Davos, "From Chatham House Man to Davos Man" alluding to, respectively, the "national" and the "global" version of international relations. The resistance to mergers and acquisitions, especially hostile takeovers, in Europe or to foreign ownership and control in East Asia signals a national business culture that is somewhat incompatible with the new global economic culture. I would posit that major cities contribute to denationalize the corporate elite. Whether this is good or bad is a separate issue; but it is, I believe, one of the conditions for setting in place the systems and subcultures necessary for a global economic system.

The Space Economy of the Center

What are the spatial consequences of this new economic core of activities? What is the urban form that accommodates them? Three distinct patterns are emerging in major cities and their regions in the developed countries. First, beginning in the 1980s, there was an increase in the number of firms located in the centers of major cities associated with growth in leading sectors and ancillary industries. This type of growth also took place in some of the most dynamic cities in developing countries, such as Seoul, Bangkok, Taipei, Bombay, São Paulo, Mexico City, and, toward the end of the decade, Buenos Aires. Second, along with this central city growth came the formation of dense nodes of commercial development and business activity in a broader urban region, a pattern less evident in developing countries except in the export-oriented growth poles discussed earlier. These nodes assumed different forms: suburban office complexes, **edge cities, exopoles,** urban agglomerations in peripheral areas. *Edge cities* refers to significant concentrations of offices and business activities alongside residential areas in peripheral areas that are completely connected to central locations via state-of-the-art electronic means. Thus far, these forms are only rarely evident in developing countries, where vast urban sprawl with a seemingly endless metropolitanization of the region around cities has been the norm. In developed countries, the revitalized urban center and the new regional nodes together constitute the spatial base for cities at the top of transnational hierarchies. The third pattern is the growing intensity in the "localness," or marginality, of areas and sectors that operate outside that world market-oriented subsystem, and this includes an increase in poverty and disadvantage. This general dynamic operates in cities with very diverse economic, political, social, and cultural arrangements (see Benko and Dunford 1991; Cheshire and Hay 1989; Gans 1984; Hausserman and Siebel 1987; Henderson and Castells 1987; see also Cobos 1984; Sassen 2000).

A few questions spring to mind. One question is whether the type of spatial organization characterized by dense strategic nodes spread over the broader region does or does not constitute a new form of organizing the territory of the "center," rather than, as in the more conventional view, an instance of suburbanization or geographic dispersal. Insofar as these various nodes are articulated through cyber-routes or digital highways, they represent the new geographic correlate of the most advanced type of "center." The places that fall outside this new grid of digital highways are peripheralized. We might ask whether this is so now to a much higher degree than in earlier periods, when the suburban or noncentral economic terrain was integrated into the center because it was primarily geared *to* the center.

Another question is whether this new terrain of centrality is differentiated. Basically, is the old central city, which is still the largest and densest of all the nodes, the most strategic and powerful node? Does it have a sort of gravitational power over the region that makes the new grid of nodes and digital highways cohere as a complex spatial agglomeration? From a larger transnational perspective, these are vastly expanded central regions. This reconstitution of the center is different from agglomeration patterns still prevalent in most cities that have not seen a massive expansion in their role as sites for global city functions and the new regime of accumulation it entails. We are seeing a reorganization of space/time dimensions of the urban economy (Sassen 2000).

Under these conditions, the traditional perimeter of the city, a kind of periphery, unfolds its full industrial and structural growth potential. Commercial and office space development lead to a distinct form of decentralized reconcentration of economic activity on the urban periphery. This geographic shift has much to do with the locational decisions of transnational and national firms that make the urban peripheries the growth centers of the most dynamic industries.[5] It is distinctly not the same as largely residential suburbanization or metropolitanization.

---

5. That is, edge cities, exopoles, suburban office parks.

We may be seeing a difference in the pattern of global city formation in parts of the United States and in parts of Western Europe (e.g., Fainstein 1993; Hitz et al. 1995). In the United States, major cities such as New York and Chicago have large centers that have been rebuilt many times, given the brutal neglect suffered by much urban infrastructure and the imposed obsolescence so characteristic of U.S. cities. This neglect and accelerated obsolescence produce vast spaces for rebuilding the center according to the requirements of whatever regime of urban accumulation or pattern of spatial organization of the urban economy prevails at a given time.

In Europe, urban centers are far more protected, and they rarely contain significant stretches of abandoned space; the expansion of workplaces and the need for "intelligent" buildings necessarily will have to take place partly outside the old centers. One of the most extreme cases is the complex of La Defense, the massive, state-of-the-art office complex developed right outside Paris to avoid harming the built environment inside the city. This is an explicit instance of government policy and planning aimed at addressing the growing demand for central office space of prime quality. Yet another variant of this expansion of the "center" onto hitherto peripheral land can be seen in London's Docklands. This vast and little-used harbor area in London became the site of an expensive, state-of-the-art development project that was meant to accommodate the rapidly growing demand for office space in the center. The financial and real estate crisis of the early 1990s resulted in the collapse of the project. By 1993, however, there had been a reorganization under a new consortium, a rapidly growing interest on the part of worldwide buyers that brought full occupancy of the complex. Similar projects for recentralizing peripheral areas were launched in several major cities in Europe, North America, and Japan during the late 1980s. As with the Docklands and Times Square redevelopments, many of these did not succeed until the mid- or late 1990s, after the crisis of 1990-91 was over. What was once the suburban fringe, urban perimeter, or urban periphery has now become the site for intense commercial development.

Conclusion: Concentration and the Redefinition of the Center

The central concern in this chapter was to examine the fact of locational concentration of leading sectors in urban centers. This concentration has occurred in the face of globalization of economic activity, massive increases in the volume of transactions, and revolutionary changes in technology that neutralize the meaning of distance.

A somewhat detailed empirical examination of several cases illuminates different aspects of this trend toward concentration. Miami is a city that has emerged as a significant regional site for global city functions. What is interesting about Miami is that it lacks a long history as an international banking and business center, the typical case for such global cities as New York or London. Miami allows us to see in almost laboratory-like fashion how a new international corporate sector can become implanted in a site. It allows us to understand something about the dynamics of globalization in the current period and how it is embedded in place.

The case of Toronto, a city whose financial district was built up only in recent years, allows us to see to what extent the pressure toward concentration is embedded in an economic dynamic and that it is not simply a consequence of a built infrastructure from the past, as one would expect in older centers such as London or New York. But Toronto also shows us that certain industries in particular are subject to the pressure toward spatial concentration, most notably finance and its sister industries.

The case of Sydney allows us to explore the interaction of a vast, continental economic scale and pressures toward spatial concentration. Rather than strengthening the multipolarity of the Australian urban system, the developments of the 1980s—increased internationalization of the Australian economy; sharp increases in foreign investment; a strong shift toward finance, real estate, and producer services—all contributed to a greater concentration of major economic activities and actors in Sydney. This concentration included a declining share of such activities and actors in Melbourne, long the center of commercial activity and wealth in Australia.

Finally, we examined the case of the leading financial centers in the world today to see whether their concentration of financial activity had declined given globalization of the markets and immense increases in the global volume of transactions. We found that their levels of concentration remain unchanged in the face of massive transformations in the financial industry and in the technological infrastructure this industry depends on.

But what exactly is the center in the contemporary economy, which is characterized by growing use of electronic and telecommunication capability? The final section of the chapter examined the spatial correlates of the center and posited that today there is no longer a simple, straightforward relation between centrality and such geographic entities as the downtown or the central business district. In the past, and up to quite recently in fact, the center was synonymous with the downtown or the CBD.

Today, it was argued here, the spatial correlate of the center can assume several geographic forms. It can be the CBD, as it still is largely in New York City, or it can extend into metropolitan areas in the form of a grid of nodes of intense business activity, as we see in Frankfurt.

Elsewhere (Sassen 1991), I have argued that we are also seeing the formation of a transterritorial "center" constituted via digital highways and intense economic transactions; I argued that the cross-border network of global cities can be seen as constituting such a transterritorial terrain of centrality *with regard to a specific complex of industries and activities.* At the limit, we may see terrains of centrality that are disembodied, that lack any territorial correlate, that are in the electronically generated space we call cyberspace. As was argued in an earlier chapter, certain components of the financial industry, particularly the foreign currency markets, can be seen as operating partly in cyberspace.

One of the reasons for focusing on centrality and on its spatial correlates is to recover a particular kind of place—cities—in the operation of global processes. Such a recovery of place allows us to introduce questions concerning the social order associated with some of these transformations. This is the subject of the next chapter.

6

The New Inequalities within Cities

What is the impact of the ascendance of finance and producer services on the broader social and economic structure of major cities? And what are the consequences of the new urban economy on the earnings distribution of a city's workforce? We know that when manufacturing was the leading sector of the economy, it created the conditions for the expansion of a vast middle class because (1) it facilitated unionization; (2) it was based in good part on household consumption, and hence wage levels mattered in that they created an effective demand; and (3) the wage levels and social benefits typical of the leading sectors became a model for broader sectors of the economy.

We want to know about the place of workers lacking the high levels of education required by the advanced sectors of the economy in these major cities. Have these workers become superfluous? We also want to know about the place in an advanced urban economy of firms and sectors that appear to be backward or to lack the advanced technological and human capital base of the new leading sectors. Have they also become superfluous? Or are such workers, firms, and sectors actually articulated to the economic core, but under conditions of severe segmentation in the social, economic, racial, and organizational traits of firms and workers? We want to know, finally, to what extent this segmentation is produced or strengthened by the existence of ethnic/racial segmentation in combination with racism and discrimination.

Remarkably enough, we can see general tendencies at work on the social level just as we can on the economic level. Recent research shows sharp increases in socioeconomic and spatial inequalities within major cities of the developed world. This finding can be interpreted as merely a quantitative increase in the degree of inequality, one that is not associated with the emergence of new social forms or class realignments. But it can also be interpreted as social and economic restructuring and the emergence of new social forms: (1) the growth of an informal economy in large cities in highly developed countries, (2) high-income commercial and residential gentrification, and (3) the sharp rise of homelessness in rich countries.

Our concern in this chapter is to describe the general outlines of this transformation. The nature of the subject is such that a fully adequate account would require introducing the specific conditions typical to each city, a task that falls outside the limits of this book. For that reason, too, much of the empirical background shaping some of the specific statements made here comes from the case of the United States. The reasons for focusing particularly on the United States are that there are more detailed analyses available and the trends under discussion are sharper.

The first half of the chapter discusses the transformation in the organization of the labor process, particularly as it materializes in large cities. The second half focuses on the earnings distribution in a service-dominated economy. This discussion includes somewhat more detailed accounts of the informal economy and of the restructuring of urban consumption, two key processes embedded in the changed earnings distribution.

Transformations in the Organization of the Labor Process

The consolidation of a new economic core of professional and servicing activities needs to be viewed alongside the general move to a service economy and the decline of manufacturing. New economic sectors are reshaping the job supply. So, however, are new ways of organizing work in both new and old sectors of the economy. The computer can now be used to do secretarial as well as manufacturing work. Components of the work process that even 10 years ago took place on the shop floor and were classified as production jobs today have been replaced by a combination of machine/service worker or worker/engineer. The machine in this case is typically computerized; for instance, certain operations that required a highly skilled craftsperson can now be done through computer-aided design and calibration. Activities that were once consolidated in a single-service retail establishment have now been divided between a service delivery outlet and central headquarters. Finally, much work that was once standardized mass production is today increasingly characterized by customization, flexible specialization, networks of subcontractors, and informalization, even at times including sweatshops and industrial homework. In brief, the changes in the job supply evident in major cities are a function of new sectors as well as of the reorganization of work in both the new and the old sectors.

The historical forms assumed by economic growth in the post-World War II era that contributed to the vast expansion of a middle class—notably, capital intensity, standardized production, and suburbanization-led growth—deterred and reduced systemic tendencies toward inequality by constituting an economic regime centered on mass production and mass consumption. (Furthermore, so did the cultural forms accompanying these processes, particularly as they shaped the structures of everyday life insofar as a large middle class contributes to mass consumption and thus to standardization in production.) These various trends led to greater levels of unionization and other forms of workers' empowerment that can be derived from large scales in production and the centrality of mass production and mass consumption in national economic growth and profits. This form of economic growth, along with government programs, contributed to reduce the number of poor in the United States (see Exhibit 6.1) and in most highly developed economies.

It was also in that postwar period extending into the late 1960s and early 1970s that the incorporation of workers into formal labor market relations reached its highest level in the most advanced economies. The formalization of the employment relation carries with it the implementation (albeit frequently precarious) of a set of regulations that have had the overall effect of protecting workers and securing the fruits of frequently violent labor struggles. (But this formalization also entailed the exclusion of distinct segments of the workforce, particularly in certain heavily unionized industries.)

The economic and social transformations in the economy since the mid-1970s assume specific forms in urban labor markets. Changes in the functioning of urban labor markets since the mid-1970s have a number of possible origins. The most evident of these changes stem from the long-term shifts in the occupational and industrial balance of employment, which directly affects the mix of job characteristics, including earnings levels and employment stability, and the types of careers available to local workers. On the demand side, these developments include the new flexibility that employers have tended to seek under the pressure of international competition, unstable product markets, and a weakening of political support for public sector programs. This new flexibility tends to mean more part-time and temporary jobs. On the supply side, a key factor has been the persistence of high unemployment in the 1970s and 1980s in many large cities, which notably altered the bargaining position of employers, and the insecurity or marginalization of the most disadvantaged

EXHIBIT 6.1

The Number of Poor People in the United States, 1970 to 1997 (thousands)

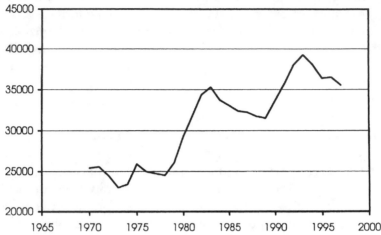

Source: Based on U.S. Department of Commerce, *Measuring 50 Years of Economic Change* (1998:Table C-22).

groups in the labor market. Workers desperate for jobs in the 1980s became willing to take increasingly unattractive jobs. In combination, these major developments on the two sides of the labor market, all of which have operated most strongly in the urban core, seem likely to have induced, on the one hand, a growing destabilization of employment with increasing casualization and/or informalization of jobs and, on the other hand, an increasing polarization of employment opportunities with new types of social divisions.

Metropolitan labor markets will tend to reflect a variety of background factors beyond particular restructuring effects. The most important include their sheer size and density, the particular industrial and occupational mix of their employment base, the overall state of tightness or slack in labor demand, and in many cities, the presence and characteristics of immigrant groups. Two characteristics of the labor markets in major cities today (as well as a century ago) are the fluidity and openness that influence the types of activity prospering there, as well as the labor market experiences of their residents. But equally important is the fact that the labor markets in and around the cities are *structured* with particular sets of jobs having attached to them distinctive combinations of rewards, security, and conditions of access (see Gordon and Sassen 1992).

The labor market characteristics of many important industries in major cities evince tendencies toward shorter-term employment relationships. Whether it is fashion-oriented industries such as the garment trade, private consumer services, trades historically associated with mass production, or the current speculative financial services, a significant share of establishments operate in competitive and often highly unstable markets. Again the evidence is that turnover rates in these activities are much higher than in large establishments and in monopolistic, bureaucratized organizations. And one of the attractions of cities for these more unstable activities must be the ease with which employment levels can be adjusted up and down because of fluid labor markets.

High rates of turnover also have implications on the supply side, adding to the attractions of the city for speculative migrants, particularly for minorities who have difficulty gaining access to more closed sectors of employment and for young single workers for whom job security may be a lower priority. The availability of these particular labor supplies must then have further implications for employers' strategies. The actual structure of urban labor markets has been more complex and changeable than agglomeration economies and the "natural selection" of activities and groups of workers can account for. The rapid growth in unemployment levels in many European cities captures the overall outcome of these various processes (see Exhibit 6.2). The European case is particularly interesting because it has a stronger tradition of government protection of workers.

The potential importance of the presence or absence of a large immigrant labor force extends to a range of issues, including the level of wages in the lower part of the labor market and its implications for the cost of living and the competitiveness of local activities, as well as for patterns of segmentation and opportunities of advancement for indigenous workers. Furthermore, given the typical concentration of new migrants in central cities, immigration has also contributed to changes in spatial patterns in labor supply. In the United States, there has also been a marked decentralization of the white population into the outer rings of the metropolitan regions; in major cities, white flight to the suburbs was counterbalanced by mostly Third World immigration into urban centers from the mid-1970s on.

Trends toward concentration of immigrants and ethnic populations in the center are also evident in other major cities in the developed world, from the well-known case of London to the little-known one of Tokyo. Thus, in 1991, Greater London had 1.35 million residents, or 20% of the population, classified as ethnic minorities. Ethnic minorities were 25.7%

EXHIBIT 6.2

Unemployment in Select European Cities, 1980 and 1990 (percentages)

City	Unemployment	
	1980	*1990*
Amsterdam	8.2	19.5 (1988)
Barcelona	15.5 (1981)	14.6 (1988)
Birmingham	15	10.3
Brussels	6	16.7 (1989)
Copenhagen	7.8	11.3 (1988)
Dortmund	5.7	11.9
Dublin	9.9	18.4 (1987)
Glasgow	8	15
Hamburg	3.2	11.2
Liverpool	16	20
Lyons	6.1	8.3
Madrid	12	12.5
Marseilles	12.2	18.1
Milan	5.5 (1981)	5.0 (1989)
Montpellier	6.8	10.3
Naples	14.5	23
Paris	7	8.4
Rennes	8.1	10.1
Rotterdam	8.8	17.1 (1988)
Seville	18.7	25.2
Valencia	9.9	17.5

Source: Based on European Institute of Urban Affairs, *Urbanisation and the Functions of Cities in the European Community: A Report to the Commission of the European Communities, Directorate General for Regional Policy (XVI) (1992:83-87).*

of the population of Inner London and about 17% in Outer London. Some of London's inner boroughs have extremely high concentrations: Brent about 45%, Newham over 42%, and Tower Hamlets over 35%. Thus, we see here a very high degree of spatial segregation and heavy concentration in central urban areas. These conditions did not change much in the 1990s.

In Tokyo, 250,000 foreign residents were officially registered in 1991. This figure is an understatement because it excludes the growing illegal immigration (see Morita 1993; Sassen 1998:chap. 4). But also in Tokyo we see a pattern of spatial concentration in the center of the city. Thus, 85% of these registered foreigners were living in central Tokyo with a disproportionate share, especially those of Asian origin, concentrated in a few small areas in the center of the city. Although the registered foreign population represents a mere 2.3% of the total population of central Tokyo, its share rises to 5% in the center of the city. As in London, this is right next to the general area that houses the financial institutions and the headquarters of important Japanese and foreign firms (Sassen 1998); it is the national and international business and financial heart of the Japanese economy. Furthermore, in some of the areas in the inner city where Asians are concentrated—and, it is known, where many of the unregistered, undocumented new immigrants live—foreigners account for a much larger proportion of residents. In Shinjuku ward, the new site of the city's government and a major commercial center, there are sections where foreigners account for 15 to 20% of all residents: Kabukicho and Ohkubo are examples (Sonobe 1993). About two-thirds of these foreigners are Korean and Chinese, but there are also rapidly growing numbers of foreigners from other Asian countries.

The expansion of low-wage jobs as a function of growth trends implies a reorganization of the capital/labor relation. To see this effect clearly, we must distinguish the *characteristics* of jobs from their sectoral location. That is, highly dynamic, technologically advanced growth sectors may well contain low-wage, dead-end jobs. Furthermore, the distinction between sectoral characteristics and sectoral growth patterns is crucial: Backward sectors such as downgraded manufacturing or low-wage service occupations can be part of major growth trends in a highly developed economy. It is often assumed that backward sectors express decline trends. Similarly, there is a tendency to assume that advanced industries, such as finance, have mostly good, white-collar jobs when in fact they also have a significant share of low-paying jobs, from cleaners to stock clerks.

We tend to think of finance and specialized services as a matter of expertise rather than of production. High-level business services, from accounting to decision-making expertise, are not usually analyzed in terms of their production process. Thus, insufficient attention has gone to the actual array of jobs from high paying to low paying involved in the production of these services. In fact, the elaboration of a financial instrument, for example, requires inputs from law, accounting, advertising, and other specialized services. Advanced services benefit from agglomeration and show a tendency toward forming a production complex, as was discussed in Chapter 4. The production process itself, moreover, includes a variety of workers and firms not usually thought of as part of the information economy—notably, secretaries, maintenance workers, and cleaners. These latter jobs are also key components of the service economy. Thus, no matter how high the place a city occupies in the new transnational hierarchies, it will have a significant share of low-wage jobs thought of as somewhat irrelevant in an advanced information economy, even though they are an integral component.

There have been objective transformations in the forms of organizing manufacturing, with a growing presence of small-batch production, small scales, high product differentiation, and rapid changes in output. These elements have promoted subcontracting and the use of flexible ways of organizing production. Flexible forms of production, ranging from highly sophisticated to very primitive, can be found equally in advanced or in backward industries. Such ways of organizing production assume distinct forms in the labor market, in the components of labor demand, and in the conditions under which labor is employed. Indications of these changes are the decline of unions in manufacturing, the loss of various contractual protections, and the increase of involuntary, part-time, and temporary work or other forms of contingent labor. An extreme indication of this downgrading is the growth of sweatshops and industrial homework.

The expansion of a downgraded manufacturing sector partly involves the same industries that used to have largely organized plants and reasonably well-paid jobs, but it replaces these with different forms of production and organization of the work process, such as piecework and industrial homework. But it also involves new kinds of activity associated with the new major growth trends. The possibility for manufacturers to develop alternatives to the organized factory becomes particularly significant in growth sectors. The consolidation of a downgraded manufacturing sector—whether through social or technical transformation—can be seen as a politico-economic response to a need for expanded production in a situation of growing average wages and militancy (as was the case in the 1960s and early 1970s).

The Informal Economy

A good part of the downgraded manufacturing sector is an instance of **informalization,** or a component of the informal sector. Although informal sectors are thought to emerge only in Third World cities, we are now seeing rapid growth of informal work in most major cities in highly developed countries, from New York and Los Angeles to Paris and Amsterdam (Portes, Castells, and Benton 1989; Renooy 1984; Sassen 1998:chap. 8; WIACT 1993).

We need to distinguish two spheres for the circulation of goods and services produced in the informal economy. One sphere circulates internally and mostly meets the demands of its members, such as small immigrant-owned shops in the immigrant community that service the latter; the other circulates throughout the "formal" sector of the economy. In this second sphere, informalization represents a direct profit-maximizing strategy, one that can operate through subcontracting, the use of sweat-shops and homework, or direct acquisition of goods or services. We are seeing not only increasingly downgraded manufacturing but also down-graded mass consumer services, whether public or private, alongside in-creasingly upgraded nonmass consumer services.

These conditions suggest that the combination of several trends partic-ularly evident in major cities present inducements to informalization: (1) the increased demand for highly priced customized services and products by the expanding high-income population, (2) the increased demand for extremely low-cost services and products by the expanding low-income population, (3) the demand for customized services and goods or limited runs from firms that are either final or intermediate buyers with a corre-sponding growth of subcontracting, (4) the increasing inequality in the bidding power of different types of firms in a context of acute pressures on land because of the rapid growth and strong agglomerative pattern of the leading industries, and (5) the continuing demand by various firms and sectors of the population—including demand from leading industries and high-income workers—for goods and services typically produced in firms with low profit rates that find it increasingly difficult to survive above-ground, given rising rents and production costs.

The transformation of final and intermediate consumption and the growing inequality in the bidding power of firms and households create inducements for informalization in a broad range of activities and spheres of the economy. The existence of an informal economy in turn emerges as a mechanism for reducing costs, even in the case of firms and households that do not need it for survival, and for providing flexibility in instances where this is essential or advantageous (Sassen 1998:chap. 8).

The Earnings Distribution in a Service-Dominated Economy

What we want to know next is the impact that these various shifts have had on the earnings distribution and income structure in a service-domi-nated economy. A growing body of studies on the occupational and earn-ings distribution in service industries finds that services produce a larger share of low-wage jobs than manufacturing does, although the latter may increasingly be approaching parity with services; moreover, several major service industries also produce a larger share of jobs in the highest-paid occupations (Economic Policy Institute 1998; Goldsmith and Blakely 1992; Harrison and Bluestone 1988; Nelson and Lorence 1985; Sheets, Nord, and Phelps 1987; Silver 1984; Stanback and Noyelle 1982).

Much scholarly attention has been focused on the importance of manufacturing in reducing income inequality in the 1950s and 1960s (Blumberg 1981; Stanback et al. 1981). Central reasons typically identified for this effect are the greater productivity and higher levels of unionization found in manufacturing. Clearly, however, these studies tend to cover a period largely characterized by such conditions, and since that time, the organization of jobs in manufacturing has undergone pronounced transformation. In what was at the time a major breakthrough and the most detailed analysis of occupational and industry data, Harrison and Bluestone (1988) found that earnings in manufacturing have declined in many industries and occupations. This type of analysis has not been replicated with more updated data sets. Glickman and Glasmeier (1989) found that a majority of manufacturing jobs in the Sunbelt are low wage, and Fernandez-Kelly and Sassen (1992) found growth of sweatshops and homework in several industry branches in New York and Los Angeles.

A considerable number of studies with a strong theoretical bent (Hill 1989; Lipietz 1988; Massey 1984; Sassen 1988; Scott and Storper 1986) argue that the declining centrality of mass production in national growth and the shift to services as the leading economic sector contributed to the demise of a broader set of arrangements. In the postwar period, the economy functioned according to a dynamic that transmitted the benefits accruing to the core manufacturing industries onto more peripheral sectors of the economy. The benefits of price and market stability and increases in productivity could be transferred to a secondary set of firms, including suppliers and subcontractors, but also to less directly related industries. Although there was still a vast array of firms and workers that did not benefit from the shadow effect, their number was probably at a minimum in the postwar period. By the early 1980s, the wage-setting power of leading manufacturing industries and this shadow effect had eroded significantly (see Exhibits 6.3 and 6.4).

Scholarship on the impact of services on the income structure of cities is only now beginning to emerge in most countries. There are now several detailed analyses of the social impact of service growth in major metropolitan areas in the United States (Fainstein et al. 1992; Nelson and Lorence 1985; Ross and Trachte 1983; Sheets, Nord, and Phelps 1987; Stanback and

EXHIBIT 6.3

Share of Aggregate Income Received by Each Fifth and Top 5% of Families in the United States, 1970 and 1997 (percentages)

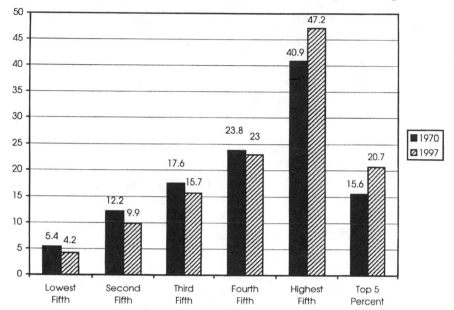

Source: Based on the U.S. Bureau of the Census, 1997.

Noyelle 1982). Sheets, Nord, and Phelps (1987) found that from 1970 to 1980 several service industries had a significant effect on the growth of underemployment, which they define as employment paying below poverty-level wages in the 199 largest metropolitan areas. The strongest effect was associated with the growth of producer services and retail trade. The highest relative contribution resulted from what the authors call "corporate services" (FIRE [finance, insurance, and real estate], business services, legal services, membership organizations, and professional services), such that a 1% increase in employment in these services was found to result in a 0.37% increase in full-time, year-round, low-wage jobs. Furthermore, a 1% increase in distributive services resulted in a 0.32% increase in full-time, year-round, low-wage jobs. In contrast, a 1% increase in personal services was found to result in a 0.13% increase in such full-time jobs and a higher share of part-time, low-wage jobs. The retail industry had the highest effect on the creation of part-time, year-round, low-wage jobs, such that a 1% increase in retail employment was found to result in a 0.88% increase in such jobs.

EXHIBIT 6.4

Real Average Weekly and Hourly Earnings of Production and Nonsupervisory Workers in the United States, 1967 to 1998 (US$)

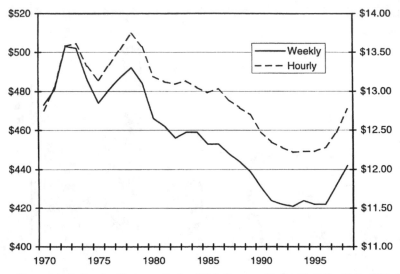

Source: Economic Policy Institute analysis of *U.S. Bureau of Labor Statistics Data* (U.S. Bureau of Labor 1998).

But what about the impact of services on the expansion of high-income jobs? Nelson and Lorence (1985) examined this question using census data on the 125 largest urban areas. To establish why male earnings are more unequal in metropolises with high levels of service sector employment, they measured the ratio of median earnings over the 5th percentile to identify the difference in earnings between the least affluent and the median metropolitan male earners; and they measured the ratio at the 95th percentile to establish the gap between median and affluent earners. Overall, they found that inequality in the 125 areas appeared to be the result of greater earnings disparity between the highest and the median earners than between the median and lowest earners (Nelson and Lorence 1985:115). Furthermore, they found that the strongest effect came from the producer services and that the next strongest was far weaker (social services in 1970 and personal services in 1980). What had been only dimly perceived and discarded by many as measurement quirks, became a full-blown reality in the 1990s. The growth in the share of income going to the top fifth of families in the United States grew while other sectors of the population lost share (see Exhibit 6.3), average hourly wages of workers with top levels of education grew while those of workers with lower levels fell (see Exhibits 6.4 and 6.5), and household income grew increasingly unequal (see Exhibit 6.6).

The conditions for ongoing inequality can also be seen in projections for educational requirements. In the United States, the evidence for 1988 shows that 17% of jobs required less than a high school diploma and over 40% would require only a high school diploma. Only about 22% of jobs required at least a college degree. By the year 2000, the expectation is that there will be very little change in these levels, with 16.5% of jobs requiring less than high school and only 22.9% requiring at least a college degree. That is to say, by the year 2000 over half of all jobs will require only a high school diploma or less. The change is somewhat sharper when we consider only net new jobs, with only 13% of jobs requiring less than high school and almost 30% requiring at least a college degree (Bailey 1990). The expansion of low-wage service jobs in large cities and the downgrading of many manufacturing jobs suggest that a good share of jobs in cities will be among those requiring only a high school education or less.

In their own distinct form, these trends are evident in many highly developed countries (Brosnan and Wilkinson 1987; Cheshire and Hay 1989; Mingione 1991). Of interest here is Japan, since little seems to be known or reported in general commentaries about growing casualization of employment. We now turn to a brief description of the growth of service jobs in Japan.

The Growth of Low-Wage Jobs in Japan

Japan also has seen considerable growth of low-wage service jobs, the replacement of many full-time male workers with part-time female workers, and the growth of forms of subcontracting that weaken the claims of workers on their firms. Over half of the new jobs created in Tokyo in the 1980s were part-time or temporary jobs.

There are other indications of structural change in Japan in the 1980s. Since the mid-1980s, average real earnings in Japan have been decreasing, and the manufacturing sector has been losing its wage-setting influence. Furthermore, with few exceptions, most of the service industries that *are* growing have significantly lower average earnings than do manufacturing, transport, and communications. Hotel and catering had among the lowest average earnings, along with health services and retail. Many of

EXHIBIT 6.5

Average Real Hourly Wages of All Workers, by Education in the United States, 1973 to 1997 (1997 Dollars)

Year	Less Than High School	High School	Some College	College	Advanced Degree
1973	$11.21	$12.82	$14.16	$18.60	$22.67
1974	$10.96	$12.48	$13.62	$18.02	$23.03
1975	$10.65	$12.38	$13.68	$17.87	$23.00
1976	$10.85	$12.48	$13.88	$17.77	$22.37
1977	$10.91	$12.38	$13.47	$17.56	$22.31
1978	$10.76	$12.40	$13.66	$17.55	$22.22
1979	$11.15	$12.49	$13.61	$17.43	$21.42
1980	$10.80	$12.07	$13.34	$17.16	$20.98
1981	$10.55	$11.91	$13.22	$17.20	$20.85
1982	$10.31	$11.90	$13.18	$17.41	$21.39
1983	$10.12	$11.78	$13.07	$17.48	$21.82
1984	$10.00	$11.66	$13.20	$17.68	$22.22
1985	$ 9.91	$11.70	$13.33	$17.95	$22.66
1986	$ 9.91	$11.72	$13.32	$17.66	$21.90
1987	$ 9.71	$11.65	$13.28	$17.73	$21.94
1988	$ 9.63	$11.59	$13.09	$17.56	$21.80
1989	$ 9.38	$11.36	$13.19	$17.88	$23.24
1990	$ 9.15	$11.18	$13.19	$18.00	$23.30
1991	$ 8.99	$11.13	$13.07	$17.69	$23.55
1992	$ 8.86	$11.07	$12.52	$18.04	$23.03
1993	$ 8.72	$11.02	$12.47	$17.97	$23.22
1994	$ 8.52	$11.10	$12.36	$18.14	$24.17
1995	$ 8.25	$10.90	$12.20	$18.13	$23.90
1996	$ 8.21	$10.84	$12.18	$17.86	$23.80
1997	$ 8.22	$11.02	$12.43	$18.38	$24.07

Note: Values are adjusted for inflation using the CPI-U-X1 deflator.

Source: Economic Policy Institute analysis of U.S. Bureau of the Census, Current Population Survey data, 1998 (http://www.census.gov).

the industries that are growing either pay above-average wages—as in finance, insurance, and real estate—or pay below-average wages. The same

EXHIBIT 6.6

Percentage of Change in Household Gini Coefficients in the United States, 1967 to 1997

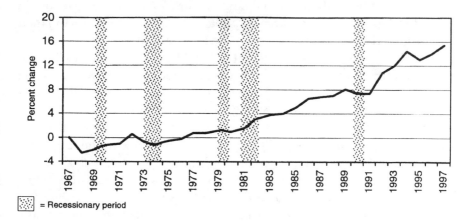

= Recessionary period

Source: U.S. Department of Commerce, "Money Income in the U.S.: 1997" (1998).

trends found in many Western cities are becoming evident in Tokyo. (For a full discussion, see Sassen 1991:chaps. 8, 9; Cybriwsky 1991.)

Data from the Labor Force Survey in Japan show that the share of part-time workers increased from under 7% of all workers in 1970 to 19.5% in 1996, or 10.5 million workers. Among female workers, this share almost doubled, from about 12% in 1970 to 22% in 1985 and 34% in 1996, or a total of about 6.92 million women.[1] As of 1996, manufacturing (19.6%), wholesale/retail and eating/drinking establishments (30.6%) and services (30.3%) had the highest share of part-time workers, an indication of the growth of a casualized employment relation in those sectors.

By the late 1980s, 58% of all firms surveyed employed part-time workers. By the late 1980s, 58% of all firms surveyed employed part-time workers. Certain industries, mostly in the low-wage service sector, have considerably higher ratios, with "hamburger shops" at 89%, labor provision services at 79%, and western restaurants at 71%, to name the top three. Part-time work in Japan is defined by the Ministry of Labor as a job with scheduled hours per week "substantially shorter than those of regular workers." Seasonal and temporary employment, by this definition, are ex-

---

1. All these figures exclude people employed in agriculture and forestry. Of 3.6 million female part-time workers, about 0.8 million were in manufacturing; 1.3 million in wholesale and retail trade; 170,000 in finance, insurance, and real estate; and almost 1 million in service industries (see Sassen 1991).

cluded but the prevailing characteristic of all part-time work is the lack of various benefits and entitlements, or in the terms used here, a *casualized* employment relation.

Of interest also is the situation of homeworkers, a growing category in most developed countries. Official counts of legal homeworkers in Japan show gradual decline over the last decade. In 1987, there were over 1 million such workers, almost all women (Japan Ministry of Labor 1987). The largest share of homework, 34%, is in clothing and related items, followed by 18.6% in electrical/electronic equipment (including assembly of electronic parts), and almost 16% in textiles. The remaining share includes a very broad range of activities, from making toys and lacquerware to printing and related work. Official figures describe a decline in the fully entitled share of homeworkers but possibly do not register an absolute increase among homeworkers with no protection. There are some indications that the latter category may be increasing (Sassen 1991:chap. 9).

The growth of low-wage and part-time jobs is likely to facilitate the employment of illegal immigrants. In Japan, where immigration, both legal and illegal, is not part of the cultural heritage as it is in the United States, there is now a growing illegal immigration from several Asian countries. The evidence on detected illegal immigrants from the Ministry of Justice analyzed by Morita (1990) shows that over 80% of men apprehended from 1987 to 1990 held construction and factory jobs. Clearly, factories and construction sites lend themselves to apprehension activity, unlike small service operations in the center of Tokyo or Osaka. Thus, we cannot assume that this level is an adequate representation of the occupational distribution of illegal immigrants; but it does indicate that factories are employing illegal immigrants.

According to a study of illegal immigrant employment in the major urban areas in Japan carried out by the Immigration Office of the Ministry of Justice, factories employing illegal immigrants are in a broad range of branches: metal processing, plastic processing, printing and binding, plating, press operating, materials coating. Most recently a growing number of women have been apprehended in factories in metals and plastic processing and in auto parts manufacturing (Morita 1990). Most illegal immigrants were found in medium-size and small factories. The figures for 1991 point to a continuation of these patterns; almost half of illegals detected by the government were in construction, followed by 14% in manufacturing and certain jobs in the retail industry, in particular back-room jobs in restaurants.

Estimates about the evolution of illegal immigration for unskilled jobs vary considerably, but all point to growing demand. The Ministry of Labor estimates the labor shortage will reach half a million by the end of the decade. Japan's most powerful business organization, Keidaren, puts the shortage at 5 million. Specialists estimate the shortage will range between 1 and 2 million by the year 2000. Well into the 1990s, the largest shortages are in manufacturing, particularly small- and medium-size firms. But there is considerable agreement that the service sector will be a major source of new shortages. As the current generation of Japanese employees in low-skill service jobs retires and young highly educated Japanese reject these jobs, there may well be a gradual acceptance of immigrant workers. Although later than most advanced economies, Japan now has a growing labor demand for low-wage, unskilled jobs in a context where Japanese youth are rejecting such jobs.

The Restructuring of Urban Consumption

The rapid growth of industries with a strong concentration of high- and low-income jobs has assumed distinct forms in the consumption structure, which in turn has a feedback effect on the organization of work and the types of jobs being created. In the United States, the expansion of the high-income workforce in conjunction with the emergence of new cultural forms has led to a process of high-income gentrification that rests, in the last analysis, on the availability of a vast supply of low-wage workers. As I have argued at great length elsewhere, high-income gentrification is labor intensive, in contrast to the typical middle-class suburb that represents a capital-intensive process: tract housing, road and highway construction, dependence on private automobiles or commuter trains, marked reliance on appliances and household equipment of all sorts, large shopping malls with self-service operations. Directly and indirectly, high-income gentrification replaces much of this capital intensity with workers. Similarly, high-income residents in the city depend to a much larger extent on hired maintenance staff than does the middle-class suburban home, with its concentrated input of family labor and machinery.

Although far less dramatic than in large cities in the United States, the elements of these patterns are also evident in many major Western European cities and, to some extent, in Tokyo. For instance, there has been considerable change in the occupational composition of residents in central Tokyo. Not unlike what we have seen in other major cities, there is a tendency for growing numbers of upper-level professional workers and of low-level workers to live in central cities: Sonobe (1993) found that the share of the former grew from 20% of all workers in 1975 to over 23% in 1985, and (although difficult to measure) we know that the numbers of low-wage legal and undocumented immigrants also grew and certainly have grown sharply since then. The share of middle-level workers, on the other hand, fell: For instance, the share of skilled workers fell from 16% in 1975 to 12% in 1985. Similar patterns hold for other areas of the city (Sonobe 1993). The total size of the resident workforce stayed the same, at about 4.3 million in 1975 and in 1985. We know that there was a sharp growth of high-income professional and managerial jobs in the second half of the 1980s, which could only have reinforced this trend.

The growth of the high-income population in the resident and commuting workforce has contributed to changes in the organization of the production and delivery of consumer goods and services. Behind the delicatessens and specialty boutiques that have replaced many self-service supermarkets and department stores lies a very different organization of work from that prevalent in large, standardized establishments. This difference in the organization of work is evident both in the retail and in the production phase (Gershuny and Miles 1983; Sassen 1998:chaps. 7, 8). High-income gentrification generates a demand for goods and services that are frequently not mass produced or sold through mass outlets. Customized production, small runs, specialty items, and fine food dishes are generally produced through labor-intensive methods and sold through small, full-service outlets. Subcontracting part of this production to low-cost operations and to sweatshops or households is common. The overall outcome for the job supply and the range of firms involved in this production and delivery is rather different from that characterizing the large department stores and supermarkets. There, mass production is prevalent, and hence, large standardized factories located outside of the region are the norm. Proximity to stores is of far greater importance with customized producers. Mass production and mass distribution outlets facilitate unionizing (see Sayer and Walker 1992).

The magnitude of the expansion of high-income workers and the high levels of spending contribute to this outcome. All major cities have long had a core of wealthy residents or commuters. By itself, however, this core of wealthy people could not have created the large-scale residential and commercial gentrification in the city. As a stratum, the new high-income workers are to be distinguished from this core of wealthy residents. The former's disposable income is generally not enough to make them into major investors. It is, however, sufficient for a significant expansion in the demand for highly priced goods and services—that is, to create a sufficiently large demand so as to ensure economic viability for the producers and providers of such goods and services. Furthermore, the level of disposable income is also a function of lifestyle and demographic patterns, such as postponing having children and larger numbers of two-earner households.

The expansion in the low-income population has also contributed to the proliferation of small operations and the move away from large-scale standardized factories and large chain stores for low-price goods. In good part, the consumption needs of the low-income population are met by manufacturing and retail establishments that are small, rely on family labor, and often fall below minimum safety and health standards. Cheap, locally produced sweatshop garments, for example, can compete with low-cost Asian imports. A growing number of products and services ranging from low-cost furniture made in basements to "gypsy cabs" and family day care is available to meet the demand for the growing low-income population (see Komlosy et al. 1997; Renooy 1984; Sassen 1998:chap. 8).

There are numerous instances of how the increased inequality in earnings reshapes the consumption structure and how this reshaping in turn has feedback effects on the organization of work. Some examples are the creation of a special taxi line for Wall Street that services only the financial district and an increase of "gypsy" cabs in low-income neighborhoods not serviced by regular cabs; the increase in highly customized woodwork in gentrified areas and low-cost informal rehabilitation in poor neighborhoods; the increase of homeworkers and sweatshops making either very expensive designer items for boutiques or very cheap products.

Conclusion: A Widening Gap

Developments in cities cannot be understood in isolation from fundamental changes in the larger organization of advanced economies. The combination of economic, political, and technical forces that has contributed to the decline of mass production as the central driving element in the economy brought about a decline in a broader institutional framework that shaped the employment relation. The group of service industries that constitute the driving economic force in the 1980s and into the 1990s is characterized by greater earnings and occupational dispersion, weak unions, and a growing share of unsheltered jobs in the lower-paying echelons, along with a growing share of high-income jobs. The associated institutional framework shaping the employment relation diverges from the earlier one. This new framework contributes to a reshaping of the sphere of social reproduction and consumption, which in turn has a feedback effect on economic organization and earnings. Whereas in the earlier period this feedback effect contributed to reproduce the middle class, currently, it re-produces growing earnings disparity, labor market casualization, and consumption restructuring.

All these trends are operating in major cities, in many cases with greater intensity than in medium-size towns. This greater intensity can be rooted in at least three conditions. First is the locational concentration of major growth sectors with either sharp earnings dispersion or dispropor-tionate concentration of either low- or high-paying jobs in major cities. Second is a proliferation of small, low-cost service operations made possi-ble by the massive concentration of people in such cities, in addition to a large daily inflow of nonresident workers and tourists. The ratio between the number of these service operations and the resident population is probably significantly higher in a very large city than in an average city. Furthermore, the large concentration of people in major cities tends to cre-ate intense inducements to open up such operations, as well as intense competition and very marginal returns. Under such conditions, the cost of labor is crucial, and hence the likelihood of a high concentration of low-wage jobs increases. Third, for these same reasons together with other components of demand, the relative size of the downgraded manu-facturing sector and the informal economy would tend to be larger in big cities such as New York or Los Angeles than in average-size cities.

The overall result is a tendency toward increased economic polariza-tion. When we speak of polarization in the use of land, in the organization of labor markets, in the housing market, and in the consumption struc-ture, we do not necessarily mean that the middle class is disappearing. We are rather referring to a dynamic whereby growth contributes to inequal-ity rather than to expansion of the middle class, as was the case in the two decades after World War II in the United States and the United Kingdom, and into the 1970s in Japan. In many of these cities, the middle class repre-sents a significant share of the population and hence represents an impor-tant channel through which income and lifestyle coalesce into a social form.

The middle class in the United States is a very broad category. It con-tains prosperous segments of various recent immigrant populations as well as established ethnic communities in large cities. What we can detect beginning in the 1980s is that certain segments of the middle class gain in-come and earnings, becoming wealthier while others become poorer. In brief, we see a segmenting of the middle class that has a sharper upward and downward slant than has been the case in other periods. The argu-ment put forth here is that while the middle strata still constitute the ma-jority, the conditions that contributed to their expansion and politico-economic power—the centrality of mass production and mass consumption in economic growth and profit realization—have been displaced by new sources of growth. This is not simply a quantitative transformation; we see here the elements for a new economic regime.

The growth of service employment in cities and the evidence of the associated growth of inequality raises questions about how fundamental a change this shift entails. Several of these questions concern the nature of service-based urban economies. The observed changes in the occupational and earnings distribution are outcomes not only of industrial shifts but also of changes in the organization of firms and of labor markets. A detailed analysis of service-based urban economies shows that there is considerable articulation of firms, sectors, and workers that may appear to have little connection to an urban economy dominated by finance and specialized services but in fact fulfills a series of functions that are an integral part of the urban economy. They do so, however, under conditions of sharp social, earnings, and often racial/ethnic segmentation.

7

A New Geography of Centers and Margins
Summary and Implications

Three important developments over the last 25 years laid the foundation for the analysis of cities in the world economy presented in this book. They are captured in the three broad propositions organizing the preceding chapters.

1. *The territorial dispersal of economic activities, of which globalization is one form, contributes to the growth of centralized functions and operations.* We find here a new logic for agglomeration and key conditions for the renewed centrality of cities in advanced economies. Information technologies, often thought of as neutralizing geography, actually contribute to spatial concentration. They make possible the geographic dispersal and simultaneous integration of many activities. But the particular conditions under which such facilities are available have promoted centralization of the most advanced users in the most advanced telecommunications centers. We see parallel developments in cities that function as regional nodes—that is, at smaller geographic scales and lower levels of complexity than global cities.
2. *Centralized control and management over a geographically dispersed array of economic operations does not come about inevitably as part of a "world system."* It requires the production of a vast range of highly specialized services, telecommunications infrastructure, and industrial services. Major cities are centers for the servicing and financing of international trade, investment, and headquarters operations. And in this sense, they are strategic production sites for today's leading economic sectors. This function is reflected in the ascendance of these activities in their economies. Again, cities that serve as regional centers exhibit similar developments. This is the way in which the spatial effects of the growing service intensity in the organization of all industries materialize in cities.

3. *Economic globalization has contributed to a new geography of centrality and marginality.* This new geography assumes many forms and operates in many terrains, from the distribution of telecommunications facilities to the structure of the economy and of employment. Global cities become the sites of immense concentrations of economic power while cities that were once major manufacturing centers suffer inordinate declines; highly educated workers see their incomes rise to unusually high levels while low- or medium-skilled workers see theirs sink. Financial services produce superprofits while industrial services barely survive.

Let us look more closely now at this last and most encompassing of the propositions.

The Locus of the Peripheral

The sharpening distance between the extremes evident in all major cities of developed countries raises questions about the notion of "rich" countries and "rich" cities. It suggests that the geography of centrality and marginality, which in the past was seen in terms of the duality of highly developed and less developed countries, is now also evident within developed countries and especially within their major cities.

One line of theorization posits that the intensified inequalities described in the preceding chapters represent a transformation in the geography of center and periphery. They signal that peripheralization processes are occurring inside areas that were once conceived of as "core" areas—whether at the global, regional, or urban level—and that alongside the sharpening of peripheralization processes, centrality has also become sharper at all three levels.

The condition of being peripheral is installed in different geographic terrains depending on the prevailing economic dynamic. We see new forms of peripheralization at the center of major cities in developed countries not far from some of the most expensive commercial land in the world: "inner cities" are evident not only in the United States and large European cities, but also now in Tokyo (Komori 1983; Nakabayashi 1987; KUPI [Kobe Urban Problems Institute] 1981; Sassen 1991:chap. 9). Furthermore, we can see peripheralization operating at the center in organizational terms as well (Sassen-Koob 1982; Wilson 1987). We have long known about segmented labor markets, but the manufacturing decline and the kind of devaluing of nonprofessional workers in leading industries that we see today in these cities go beyond segmentation and in fact represent an instance of peripheralization.

Furthermore, the new forms of growth evident at the urban perimeter also mean crisis: violence in the immigrant ghetto of the *banlieues* (the French term for *suburbs*), exurbanites clamoring for control over growth to protect their environment, new forms of urban governance (Body-Gendrot 1993; Pickvance and Preteceille 1991). The regional mode of regulation in many of these cities is based on the old center/suburb model and may hence become increasingly inadequate to deal with intraperipheral conflicts—conflicts between different types of constituencies at the urban perimeter or urban region. Frankfurt, for example, is a city that cannot function without its region's towns; yet this particular *urban region* would not have emerged without the specific forms of growth in Frankfurt's center. Keil and Ronneberger (1993) note the ideological motivation in the call by politicians to officially *recognize* the region so as to strengthen Frankfurt's position in the global interurban competition. This call also provides a rationale for coherence and the idea of common interests among the many objectively disparate interests in the region: It displaces the conflicts between unequally advantaged sectors onto a project of regional competition with other regions. Regionalism then emerges as the concept for bridging the global orientation of leading sectors with the various local agendas of various constituencies in the region.

In contrast, the city discourse rather than the ideology of regionalism dominates in cities such as New York or São Paulo (see Toulouse 1992). The challenge is how to bridge the inner city, or the squatters at the urban perimeter, with the center. In multiracial cities, multiculturalism has emerged as one form of this bridging. A "regional" discourse is perhaps beginning to emerge, but it has until now been totally submerged under the suburbanization banner, a concept that suggests both escape from and dependence on the city. The notion of conflict within the urban periphery between diverse interests and constituencies has not really been much of a factor in the United States. The delicate point at the level of the region has rather been the articulation between the residential suburbs and the city.

Contested Space

Large cities have emerged as strategic territories for these developments. *First, cities are the sites for concrete operations of the economy.* For our purposes, we can distinguish two forms of such concrete operations: (1) In terms of economic globalization and place, cities are strategic places that concentrate command functions, global markets, and, as demonstrated in Chapter 4, production sites for the advanced corporate service industries. (2) In terms of day-to-day work in the leading industrial complex, finance, and specialized services, we saw in Chapter 6 that a large share of the jobs involved are low paid and manual, and many are held by women and immigrants. Although these types of workers and jobs are never represented as part of the global economy, they are in fact as much a part of globalization as international finance is. We see at work here a dynamic of valorization that has sharply increased the distance between the devalorized and the valorized—indeed overvalorized—sectors of the economy. These joint presences have made cities a contested terrain.

The structure of economic activity has brought about changes in the organization of work that are reflected in a pronounced shift in the job supply, with strong polarization occurring in the income distribution and occupational distribution of workers. Major growth industries show a greater incidence of jobs at the high- and low-paying ends of the scale than do the older industries now in decline. Almost half the jobs in the producer services are lower-income jobs, and the other half are in the two highest earnings classes. On the other hand, a large share of manufacturing workers were in middle-earning jobs during the postwar period of high growth in these industries in the United States and most of western Europe.

One particular concern here was to understand how new forms of inequality actually are constituted into new social forms, such as gentrified neighborhoods, informal economies, or downgraded manufacturing sectors. To what extent these developments are connected to the consolidation of an economic complex oriented to the global market is difficult to say. Precise empirical documentation of the linkages or impacts is impossible; the effort here is focused, then, on a more general attempt to understand the consequences of both the ascendance of such an international economic complex and the general move to a service economy.

Second, the city concentrates diversity. Its spaces are inscribed with the dominant corporate culture but also with a multiplicity of other cultures and identities, notably through immigration. The slippage is evident: The dominant culture can encompass only part of the city. And while corporate power inscribes noncorporate cultures and identities with "otherness," thereby devaluing them, they are present everywhere. The immigrant communities and informal economy described in Chapter 6 are only two instances. Diverse cultures and ethnicities are especially strong in major cities in the United States and Western Europe; these also have the largest concentrations of corporate power.

We see here an interesting correspondence between great concentrations of corporate power and large concentrations of "others." It invites us to see that globalization is not only constituted in terms of capital and the new international corporate culture (international finance, telecommunications, information flows) but also in terms of people and noncorporate cultures. There is a whole infrastructure of low-wage, nonprofessional jobs and activities that constitutes a crucial part of the so-called corporate economy.

A focus on the *work* behind command functions, on *production* in the finance and services complex, and on market*places* has the effect of incorporating the material facilities underlying globalization and the whole infrastructure of jobs and workers typically not seen as belonging to the corporate sector of the economy: secretaries and cleaners, the truckers who deliver the software, the variety of technicians and repair workers, and all the jobs having to do with the maintenance, painting, and renovation of the buildings where it is all housed.

This expanded focus can lead to the recognition that a multiplicity of economies is involved in constituting the so-called global information economy. It recognizes types of activities, workers, and firms that have never been installed in the "center" of the economy or that have been evicted from that center in the restructuring of the 1980s and have therefore been devalued in a system that puts too much weight on a narrow conception of the center of the economy. Globalization can, then, be seen as a process that involves multiple economies and work cultures.

The preceding chapters have tried to demonstrate that cities are of great importance to the dominant economic sectors. Large cities in the highly developed world are the places where globalization processes assume concrete, localized forms. These localized forms are, in good part, what globalization is about. We can then think of cities also as the place where the contradictions of the internationalization of capital either come to rest or conflict. If we consider, further, that large cities also concentrate a growing share of disadvantaged populations—immigrants in both Europe and the United States, African Americans and Latinos in the United States—then we can see that cities have become a strategic terrain for a whole series of conflicts and contradictions.

On one hand, they concentrate a disproportionate share of corporate power and are one of the key sites for the overvalorization of the corporate economy; on the other, they concentrate a disproportionate share of the disadvantaged and are one of the key sites for their devalorization. This joint presence happens in a context in which (1) the internationalization of the economy has grown sharply and cities have become increasingly strategic for global capital and (2) marginalized people have come into representation and are making claims on the city as well. This joint presence is further brought into focus by the sharpening of the distance between the two. The center now concentrates immense power, a power that rests on the capability for global control and the capability to produce superprofits. And marginality, notwithstanding weak economic and political power, has become an increasingly strong presence through the new politics of culture and identity.

If cities were irrelevant to the globalization of economic activity, the center could simply abandon them and not be bothered by all of this. Indeed, this is precisely what some politicians argue—that cities have become hopeless reservoirs for all kinds of social despair. It is interesting to note again how the dominant economic narrative argues that place no longer matters, that firms can be located anywhere thanks to telematics, that major industries now are information-based and hence not place-bound. This line of argument devalues cities at a time when they are major sites for the new cultural politics. It also allows the corporate economy to extract major concessions from city governments under the notion that firms can simply leave and relocate elsewhere, which is not quite the case for a whole complex of firms, as much of this book sought to show.

In seeking to show that (1) cities are strategic to economic globalization because they are command points, global marketplaces, and production sites for the information economy and (2) many of the devalued sectors of the urban economy actually fulfill crucial functions for the center, this book attempts to recover the importance of cities specifically in a globalized economic system and the importance of those overlooked sectors that rest largely on the labor of women, immigrants, and in the case of large U.S. cities, African Americans and Latinos. In fact it is the intermediary sectors of the economy (such as routine office work, headquarters that are not geared to the world markets, the variety of services demanded by the largely suburbanized middle class) and of the urban population (the middle class) that can and have left cities. The two sectors that have stayed, the center and the "other," find in the city the strategic terrain for their operations.

Appendix

The tables in this appendix provide more detailed information about some of the issues discussed in the book. Exhibit A.1 shows the considerable variation in income levels among cities in different regions of the world. Average household payments on rent, on the other hand, show less differentiation across regions. The sharpest differences in terms of rent occur between cities in the less developed world—the difference between Johannesburg and Nairobi in Africa or between Manama and Abu Dhabi in the Middle East. Not unexpectedly, the pattern of acute international differentiation in these regions is evident in incomes for different types of work as well.

Exhibit A.2 presents information on the same cities of Exhibit A.1, adding prices and hours worked. In addition, the information in Exhibit A.2 is standardized on the levels that obtain in one particular city used as a benchmark. This city is Zurich, probably because the report where these data are presented comes from the Union Banque Suisse of Zurich. Exhibit A.2 helps us understand the differences among all the cities on the list and among the regions. It makes clear that Zurich has higher prices and wages/salaries than just about every city on the list, except Oslo, Copenhagen, and Stockholm.

Exhibit A.3 shows the changes in commercial property prices using 1994 to set the index. Four years is not a long period of time. Yet in most of these cities, the nominal price increased, with the strong exception of Tokyo where the economic crises endured through much of the 1990s. Inflation-adjusted prices show, not unexpectedly, weaker increases.

The last two tables show basic descriptive information on the largest urban agglomerations, the share of total population of a country residing in the particular city listed, and the share of the total urban population of a country residing in the city listed. The largest urban agglomerations are today overwhelmingly in Asia and Latin America. Tokyo, New York, Los Angeles, and Osaka are the only cities that are not in the developing world. The shares of a country's population residing in its top agglomeration reveal considerable variation, ranging from 33.9% in Buenos Aires to a low of under 2% in Bombay, Delhi, Calcutta, Shanghai, and Beijing. Similar marked variations are evident in the percentage of the total urban population of a country accounted for by the major cities in those countries, ranging form 38.3% in Buenos Aires to 3% in Beijing.

Exhibit A.5 shows us the list of countries that have three or more urban agglomerations with over 1 million inhabitants. In this case, the numbers are consistently higher than in the previous listing, and several of the highly developed countries appear on the list.

EXHIBIT A.1

Household Rent per Month and Gross Yearly Income, 1997 (US$)

Region/City	Normal Household Rent per Month[a]	Gross Yearly Income		
		Industrial Workers[b]	Primary School Teachers[c]	Engineers[d]
Africa				
Johannesburg	310	20,900	16,700	35,100
Nairobi	110	1,800	1,400	3,600
Central and Eastern Europe				
Budapest	270	3,300	2,600	5,100
Istanbul	360	11,600	5,400	28,900
Moscow	440	4,500	900	3,300
Prague	60	4,800	4,200	10,300
Warsaw	460	3,700	3,100	7,100
European Union				
Amsterdam	490	28,300	29,200	45,800
Athens	340	16,500	14,600	26,900
Berlin	600	28,500	36,100	47,500
Brussels	560	32,600	26,600	53,200
Copenhagen	570	39,600	38,700	55,300
Dublin	730	21,100	31,800	39,100
Frankfurt	840	34,400	41,800	65,200
Geneva	720	46,300	69,300	54,400
Helsinki	590	27,500	25,200	39,800
Lisbon	490	12,500	18,000	28,600
London	1,150	28,500	32,100	34,300
Luxembourg	870	33,700	53,400	54,100
Madrid	580	17,100	23,500	34,100
Milan	590	21,900	21,800	37,500
Oslo	590	33,800	28,800	43,200
Paris	790	22,000	21,400	50,600
Stockholm	490	27,900	27,100	37,400
Vienna	470	30,900	27,000	53,900
Zurich	830	49,800	68,800	72,500

Latin America				
Bogota	600	8,000	4,500	25,400
Buenos Aires	680	9,900	8,200	35,400
Caracas	460	4,000	5,100	7,100
Panama	500	5,800	6,000	19,500
Rio de Janeiro	750	12,500	4,200	29,400
São Paulo	840	16,800	6,500	37,400
Middle East				
Abu Dhabi	1,250	12,700	19,500	44,700
Manama	320	15,700	14,300	26,700
Tel Aviv	610	19,600	15,200	33,900
North America				
Chicago	750	38,800	42,000	38,500
Houston	500	37,100	31,500	42,500
Los Angeles	770	41,500	41,300	53,500
New York	1,070	38,600	38,200	52,000
Mexico City	420	5,200	4,500	10,600
Montreal	390	33,200	33,900	46,400
Toronto	610	40,600	38,800	44,200
Southeast Asia and Pacific Rim				
Bangkok	190	13,800	7,500	18,600
Hong Kong	1,010	22,100	24,500	45,200
Jakarta	820	8,100	1,6.50	8,200
Kuala Lampur	480	22,400	6,200	42,000
Manila	460	3,800	5,500	8,300
Mumbai	260	2,400	1,900	3,700
Seoul	1,120	20,100	22,800	25,700
Shanghai	720	2,000	1,450	3,400
Singapore	1,170	20,900	15,300	34,500
Sydney	490	20,800	29,100	39,900
Taipei	1,030	20,200	18,800	26,500
Tokyo	1,530	49,900	37,400	54,200

a. The rents quoted are for apartments built after 1975 (three rooms) with local standard and comfort in or near the city center.

b. Industrial workers are skilled with about 10 years experience and working with a large company in the metalworking industry.

c. Primary school teachers have taught in the public school system for about 10 years.

d. Engineers are employed by an industrial firm in the machinery or electrical equipment industry and have completed university studies with at least 5 years experience.

Source: Based on Union Bank of Switzerland. *Price and Earnings Around the Globe, 1997 Edition* (http://www.ubs.com/e/index/about/research/pcc/publications.Par.0028.Fil. pdf).

EXHIBIT A.2

Price and Wage Indices and Working Hours per Annum, 1997 (numbers)

City	Prices (excl. rent) (Zurich = 100)[a]	Gross Wages and Salary (Zurich = 100)[b]	Working Hours per Year[c]
Africa			
Nairobi	63.9	3.6	2,111
Johannesburg	51.4	26	2,033
Central and Eastern Europe			
Budapest	48.8	6.5	1,830
Istanbul	45.9	17.2	2,263
Moscow	85.2	6	1,875
Prague	47.8	10.9	1,976
Warsaw	50.4	8.2	1,796
European Union			
Amsterdam	74.6	58.2	1,721
Athens	66.6	33	1,815
Berlin	75	69.3	1,667
Brussels	76	68.2	1,739
Copenhagen	102.1	8.9	1,689
Dublin	77.2	51.2	1,782
Frankfurt	83.5	75.9	1,730
Geneva	96.4	97.7	1,846
Helsinki	93.9	52.2	1,757
Lisbon	57.4	25.4	1,806
London	89.8	51.6	1,839
Luxembourg	73.4	76.6	1,766
Madrid	67.6	40.3	1,798
Milan	70.9	48	1,821
Oslo	110.9	71.5	1,748
Paris	89.2	54.2	1,742
Stockholm	101.7	62.1	1,824
Vienna	79.1	61.2	1,728
Zurich	100	100	1,876
Latin America			
Bogota	59.6	15.6	2,187
Buenos Aires	70.7	25.5	2,097
Caracas	62.5	8.4	2,001
Panama	60.5	1.6	2,095
Rio de Janeiro	80.3	21.7	1,892
São Paulo	77.2	26.1	1,906
Middle East			
Abu Dhabi	82.8	29.1	2,166
Manama	67.6	24.4	1,989
Tel Aviv	75.5	34.9	2,128
North America			
Chicago	81.1	72.3	1,891
Houston	76.2	71.4	1,875
Los Angeles	78.7	76.3	1,945
New York	82.9	77.8	1,952
Mexico City	55.3	7.9	2,302

Montreal	72.6	64	1,799
Toronto	69.2	62.5	1,927
Southeast Asia and Pacific Rim			
Bangkok	66.9	14.3	2,245
Hong Kong	77.3	34.7	2,312
Jakarta	60.7	8.8	2,121
Kuala Lampur	69.6	24.3	2,157
Manila	61.5	6.8	2,238
Mumbai	42.3	4.6	2,254
Seoul	85.3	33.7	2,253
Shanghai	70.4	4.5	2,043
Singapore	97.3	30.4	2,028
Sydney	78.8	51.6	1,777
Taipei	80.5	38	2,190
Tokyo	121.7	84.5	1,799

a. Prices are based on the cost of a basket of 111 goods and services weighted by European consumer habits.

b. Hourly wages calculated on data from 12 occupations: primary school teacher, bus driver, automobile mechanic, building laborer, skilled industrial worker, department manager, bank credit clerk, secretary, department store sales woman, female industrial worker, electrical/mechanical engineer, and cook. Wage index is weighted by the share of each occupation in overall employment, share of income in overall income, and also by gender.

c. Working hours are based on 11 occupations excluding teachers.

Source: Based on Union Bank of Switzerland, *Price and Earnings Around the Globe, 1997 Edition* (http://www.ubs.com/e/index/about/research/pcc/publications.Par.0028.Fil.pdf).

EXHIBIT A.3

Commercial Property Price Index: Major Cities, 1998 (1994 = 100)

City	Nominal Price	Inflation-Adjusted Price
New York	150	136
Tokyo	59	58
Frankfurt	105	98
Paris	102	96
Milan	111	98
London	132	117
Toronto	100	94
Madrid	183	162
Amsterdam	156	144
Sydney	118	109
Zurich	84	81
Brussels	109	103
Stockholm	185	179
Copenhagen	124	115
Oslo	119	110
Helsinki	121	116
Dublin	241	222

Source: Based on Bank for International Settlements, *69th Annual Report* (1999) (http://www.bis.org).

EXHIBIT A.4

Largest Urban Agglomerations, 1996 (millions and percentages)

Urban Agglomeration	1996 Population Country (millions)	1996 Population (millions)	Population Residing in Agglomeration (% of Total)	Percentage of Total Urban Population
Urban Agglomerations with 10 million or more				
Tokyo	Japan	27.2	21.7	27.8
Mexico City	Mexico	16.9	18.2	24.8
São Paulo	Brazil	16.8	10.4	13.2
New York	United States of America	16.4	6.1	8
Bombay	India	15.7	1.7	6.1
Shanghai	China	13.7	1.1	3.6
Los Angeles	United States of America	12.6	4.7	6.1
Calcutta	India	12.1	1.3	4.7
Buenos Aires	Argentina	11.9	33.9	38.3
Seoul	Republic of Korea	11.8	26	31.5
Beijing	China	11.4	0.9	3
Lagos	Nigeria	10.9	9.5	23.4
Osaka	Japan	10.6	8.5	10.8
Delhi	India	10.3	1.1	4
Rio de Janeiro	Brazil	10.3	6.4	8.1
Karachi	Pakistan	10.1	7.2	20.8
Urban Agglomerations between 5 and 10 million				
Cairo	Egypt	9.9	15.7	34.9
Metro Manila	Philippines	9.6	13.8	25.1
Paris	France	9.6	16.4	21.9
Tianjin	China	9.6	0.8	2.5
Moscow	Russian Federation	9.3	6.3	8.2
Dhaka	Bangladesh	9.0	7.5	39.9
Jakarta	Indonesia	8.8	4.4	12.1
Istanbul	Turkey	8.2	13.3	18.8
London	United Kingdom	7.6	13.1	14.7
Chicago	United States of America	6.9	2.5	3.3
Teheran	Iran (Islamic Rep. of)	6.9	9.9	16.7
Lima	Peru	6.8	28.5	40
Bangkok	Thailand	6.7	11.4	56.2
Essen	Germany	6.5	7.9	9.2
Bogota	Colombia	6.2	17.1	23.4
Madras	India	6.1	0.6	2.4
Hong Kong	Hong Kong, China	5.9	95.2	100
Hyderabad	India	5.7	0.6	2.2
Lahore	Pakistan	5.2	3.7	10.7
Shenyang	China	5.2	0.4	1.4
Saint Petersburg	Russian Federation	5.1	3.5	4.5
Bangalore	India	5.0	0.5	1.9
Santiago	Chile	5.0	34.5	41

Source: Based on U.N. Department of Economic and Social Affairs, Population Division.
World Urbanization Prospects 1996
(http://www.undp.org/popin/wdtrends/urb/furb.htm).

EXHIBIT A.5

Countries with Three or More Urban Agglomerations (> 1 million), 1996

Urban Agglomeration (UA)	Total Number of UA	Total Percentage Residing in UA
China	49	10.9
United States	35	38.3
India	30	9.4
Brazil	14	33.2
Germany	13	40.9
Russian Federation	13	19.1
Pakistan	8	17.3
South Africa	8	29.8
Japan	6	37.8
Republic of Korea	6	52
Australia	5	58.1
Indonesia	5	8.5
Iran (Islamic Rep. of)	5	19.4
Turkey	5	25
Ukraine	5	15.6
Canada	4	35.7
Colombia	4	34.8
Italy	4	19.5
Mexico	4	27.2
United Kingdom	4	23.4
Argentina	3	40.9
Bangladesh	3	10.5
Egypt	3	23.5
France	3	20.8
Poland	3	17.4

Source: Based on U.N. Department of Economic and Social Affairs, Population Division, *World Urbanization Prospects 1996*
(http://www.undp.org/popin/wdtrends/urb/furb.htm).

References

Abreu, A., M. Cocco, C. Despradel, E. G. Michael, and A. Peguero. 1989. *Las Zonas Francas Industriales: El Exito de una Politica Economica.* Santo Domingo: Centro de Orientacion Economica.

Abu-Lughod, Janet Lippman. 1980. *Rabat: Urban Apartheid in Morocco.* Princeton, NJ: Princeton University Press.

———. 1994. *From Urban Village to "East Village": The Battle for New York's Lower East Side.* Cambridge, MA: Blackwell.

———. 1999. *New York, Chicago, Los Angeles: America's Global Cities.* Minneapolis: University of Minnesota Press.

Adrian, C. 1984. *Urban Impacts of Foreign and Local Investment in Australia.* Publication 119. Canberra: Australian Institute of Urban Studies.

Allen, John. 1999. "Cities of Power and Influence: Settled Formations." In *Unsettling Cities,* edited by John Allen, Doreen Massey, and Michael Pryke. New York: Routledge.

Allen, John, Doreen Massey, and Michael Pryke, eds. 1999. *Unsettling Cities.* London: Routledge.

Allison, Eric. 1996. "Historic Preservation in a Development-Dominated City: The Passage of New York City's Landmark Preservation Legislation." *Journal of Urban History* 22(3):350-76.

Amin, Ash, ed. 1997. *Post-Fordism.* Oxford, UK: Blackwell Publishers.

Amin, Ash and Kevin Robins. 1990. "The Re-emergence of Regional Economies? The Mythical Geography of Flexible Accumulation." *Environment and Planning D: Society and Space* 8(1):7-34.

AMPO. 1988. "Japan's Human Imports: As Capital Flows Out, Foreign Labor Flows In." Special issue of *Japan-Asia Quarterly Review* 19(1, Special issue).

Appadurai, Arjun. 1996. *Modernity at Large.* Minneapolis: University of Minnesota Press.

Arroyo, Monica, Milton Santos, Maria Adelia A. De Souze, and Francisco Capuano Scarlato, eds. 1993. *Fim De Seculo E Globalizacao.* São Paulo: Hucitet.

Ascher, François. 1995. *Metapolis ou l'avenir des villes.* Paris: Editions Odile Jacob.

Asian Women's Association. 1988. *Women from Across the Seas: Migrant Workers in Japan.* Tokyo: Asian Women's Association.

Bagnasco, Arnaldo. 1977. *Tre Italie: La Problematica Territoriale Dello Sviluppo Italiano.* Bologna: Il Mulino.

Bailey, Thomas. 1990. "Jobs of the Future and the Education They Will Require: Evidence from Occupational Forecasts." *Educational Researcher* 20(2):11-20.

Balbo, Laura and Luigi Manconi. 1990. *I Razzismi Possibili.* Milano: Feltrinelli.

Bank for International Settlements. 1992. *62nd Annual Report.* Basel, Switzerland: BIS.

————. 1998. *Central Bank Survey.* Basel, Switzerland: BIS.

————. 1999. *69th Annual Report.* Basel, Switzerland: BIS.

Bavishi, V. and H. E. Wyman. 1983. *Who Audits the World: Trends in the Worldwide Accounting Profession.* Storrs, CT: University of Connecticut, Center for Transnational Accounting and Financial Research.

Beneria, Lourdes. 1989. "Subcontracting and Employment Dynamics in Mexico City." In *The Informal Economy: Studies in Advanced and Less Developed Countries,* edited by A. Portes, M. Castells, and L. Benton. Baltimore: Johns Hopkins University Press.

Benko, Georges and Mick Dunford, eds. 1991. *Industrial Change and Regional Development: The Transformation of New Industrial Spaces.* London and New York: Belhaven/Pinter.

Berger, Suzanne and Michael J. Piore. 1980. *Dualism and Discontinuity in Industrial Societies.* New York and London: Cambridge University Press.

Berque, Augustin. 1987. *La qualite de la ville: Urbanite française, urbanite Nippone.* Tokyo: Maison Franco-Japonaise.

Bestor, Theodore. 1989. *Neighborhood Tokyo.* Stanford, CA: Stanford University Press.

Bhachu, Parminder. 1985. *Twice Immigrants.* London: Tavistock.

Bhagwati, J. 1988. *Protectionism.* Boston: MIT Press.

Bini, Paolo Calza. 1976. *Economia periferica e classi sociali.* Napoli: Liguori.

Blaschke, J. and A. Germershausen. 1989. "Migration und ethnische Beziehungen." *Nord-Sud Aktuell* 3-4 (Special issue):

Blumberg, P. 1981. *Inequality in an Age of Decline.* New York: Oxford University Press.

Bodnar, Judith. 1996. "The Post-State Socialist City: Urban Change in Budapest." Ph.D. dissertation, Department of Sociology, Johns Hopkins University: Baltimore.

Body-Gendrot, S. 1993. *Ville et violence.* Paris: Presses Universitaires de France.

Body-Gendrot, Sophie, Emmanuel Ma Mung, and Catherine Hodier, eds. 1992. "Entrepreneurs entre deux mondes: Les creations d'entreprises par les etrangers: France, Europe, Amerique du Nord." *Revue Européenne des migrations Internationales* 8(1, Special issue):5-8.

Boissevain, Jeremy. 1992. "Les entreprises ethniques aux Pays-Bas." *Revue Européenne des migrations internationales* 8(1, Special issue):97-106.

Bonacich, E., Lucie Cheng, Nora Chinchilla, Norma Hamilton, and Paul Ong, eds. 1994. *Global Production: The Apparel Industry in the Pacific Rim*. Philadelphia: Temple University Press.

Bonamy, Joel and Nicole May, eds. 1994. *Services et mutations urbaines*. Paris: Anthropos.

Bonilla, Frank, Edwin Melendez, Rebecca Morales, and Maria de los Angeles Torres, eds. 1998. *Borderless Borders*. Philadelphia: Temple University Press.

Boris, Eileen. 1994. *Home to Work*. Cambridge, UK: Cambridge University Press.

Bose, C. and E. Acosta-Belen, eds. 1995. *Women in the Latin American Development Process*. Philadelphia: Temple University Press.

Bourgeois, P. *In Search of Respect: Selling Crack in El Barrio*. Structural Analysis in the Social Sciences Series. New York: Cambridge University Press.

Boyer, Christine. 1983. *Dreaming the Rational City*. Cambridge: MIT Press.

Boyer, Robert, ed. 1986. *La flexibilite du travail en Europe*. Paris: La Découverte.

Braudel, Fernand. 1984. *The Perspective of the World*. Vol. III. London: Collins.

Brosnan, P. and F. Wilkinson. 1987. *Cheap Labour: Britain's False Economy*. London: Low Pay Unit.

Brotchie, J., M. Barry, E. Blakely, P. Hall, and P. Newton, eds. 1995. *Cities in Competition: Productive and Sustainable Cities for the 21st Century*. Melbourne: Longman Australia.

Brown, C. 1984. *Black and White Britain*. London: Heinemann.

Brusco, Sabastiano. 1986. "Small Firms and Industrial Districts: The Experience of Italy." In *New Firms and Regional Development*, edited by David Keeble and Francis Weever. London: Croom Helm.

Buck, Nick, Matthew Drennan, and Kenneth Newton. 1992. "Dynamics of the Metropolitan Economy." In *Divided Cities: New York & London in the Contemporary World*, edited by Susan Fainstein, Ian Gordon, and Michael Harloe. Oxford, UK: Blackwell.

Burgel, Guy. 1993. *La ville aujourd'hui*. Paris: Hachette, Collection Pluriel.

Canadian Urban Institute. 1993. *Disentangling Local Government Responsibilities: International Comparisons*. Urban Focus Series 93-1. Toronto: Canadian Urban Institute.

Canevari, Annapaola. 1991. "Immigrati Prima Accoglienza: E Dopo?" *Dis T Rassegna di Studi e Ricerche del Dipartimento di Scienze del Territorio del Politecnico di Milano* 9(September):53-60.

Cardew, R. V., J. V. Langdale, and D. C. Rich, eds. 1982. *Why Cities Change: Urban Development and Economic Change in Sydney*. Sydney, Australia: Allen & Unwin.

Carleial, L. and M. R. Nabuco, orgs 1989. *Transformacoes na DiviSao Inter-regional no Brasil*. São Paulo: Anpec/Caen/Cedeplar.

Castells, M. 1983. *The City and the Grassroots: A Cross-Cultural Theory of Urban Social Movements.* Berkeley: University of California Press.

―――. 1989. *The Informational City.* London: Blackwell.

Castells, M. and P. Hall. 1994. *Technopoles of the World: The Making of Twenty-First-Century Industrial Complexes.* London: Routledge.

Castells, Manuel. 1998. *The Information Age: Economy, Society, and Culture. Vol. 3: End of Millenium.* Malden/Oxford: Blackwell.

Castells, Manuel and Yuko Aoyama. 1994. "Paths Toward the Informational Society: Employment Structure in G-7 Countries, 1920-1990." *International Labour Review, Vol. 133* (1), pp. 5-33.

Castles, S. and M. Miller. 1998. *The Age of Migration: International Population Movements in the Modern World.* London: Macmillan.

Castro, Max, ed. 1999. *Free Markets, Open Societies, Closed Borders.* Coral Gables, FL: North-South Center Press.

CEMAT. 1988. *Draft European Regional Planning Strategy.* Vols. 1 and 2. Luxembourg: CEMAT.

Chaney, E. and M. Garcia Castro. 1993. *Muchacha Cachifa Criada Empleada Empregadinha Sirvienta Y . . . Mas Nada.* Caracas: Nueva Sociedad.

Chase-Dunn, C. 1984. "Urbanization in the World System: New Directions for Research." In *Cities in Transformation,* edited by M. P. Smith. Beverly Hills, CA: Sage.

Cheshire, P. C. and D. G. Hay. 1989. *Urban Problems in Western Europe.* London: Unwin Hyman.

Ciccolella, Pablo. 1998. "Territorio de Consumo: Redefinición del Espacio en Buenos Aires en el Fin de Siglo." In *Ciudades y Regiones al Avance de la Globalización,* edited by S. Sorenstein and R. Bustos Cara. UNS (Universidad Nacional del Sur), Bahia Blanca: 201-230.

City of Toronto. 1990. *Cityplan '91: Central Area Trends Report.* Toronto: City of Toronto, Planning and Development Department.

Clark, Terry Nichols and Vincent Hoffman-Martinot, ed. 1998. *The New Public Culture.* Oxford, UK: Westview.

Clavel, P. 1986. *The Progressive City.* New Brunswick, NJ: Rutgers University Press.

Cobos, Emilio Pradilla. 1984. *Contribución a la Critica de la "Teoria Urbana": Del "Espacio" a la "Crisis Urbana."* Mexico, D.F.: Universidad Autonoma Metropolitana Xochimilco.

Cohen, R. 1987. *The New Helots: Migrants in the International Division of Labour.* London: Avebury.

Cohen, Stephen S. and John Zysman. 1987. *Manufacturing Matters: The Myth of the Post-Industrial Economy.* New York: Basic Books.

Colomina, Beatriz, ed. 1992. *Sexuality & Space.* Princeton Papers on Architecture. Princeton, NJ: Princeton Architectural Press.

Colon, Alice, Marya Munoz, Neftali Garcia, and Idsa Alegria. 1988. "Trayectoria de la Participación Laboral de las Mujeres en Puerto Rico de los Años 1950 a 1985." In *Crisis, Sociedad y Mujer: Estudio Comparativo entre Paises de America 1950-1985).* Havana: Federación de Mujeres Cubanas.

Copjec, Joan and Michael Sorkin, eds. 1999. *Giving Ground.* London: Verso.

Corbridge, S. and J. Agnew. 1991. "The U. S. Trade and Budget Deficit in Global Perspective: An Essay in Geopolitical Economy." *Environment and Planning D: Society and Space 9:* 71-90.

Corbridge, Stuart, Ron Martin, and Nigel Thrift, eds. 1994. *Money Power and Space.* Oxford, UK: Blackwell.

Cornelius, Wayne A., Philip L. Martin, and James F. Hollifield, eds. 1994. *Controlling Immigration: A Global Perspective.* Stanford, CA: Stanford University Press.

Cybriwsky, R. 1991. *Tokyo. The Changing Profile of an Urban Giant.* World Cities series, edited by R. J. Johnson and P. L. Knox. London: Belhaven.

Daly, M. T. and R. Stimson. 1992. "Sydney: Australia's Gateway and Financial Capital." In *New Cities of the Pacific Rim,* edited by E. Blakely and T. J. Stimpson. Berkeley: University of California, Institute for Urban & Regional Development.

Daniels, Peter W. 1985. *Service Industries: A Geographical Appraisal.* London and New York: Methuen.

————. 1991. "Producer Services and the Development of the Space Economy." In *The Changing Geography of Advanced Producer Services,* edited by Peter W. Daniels and Frank Moulaert. London and New York: Belhaven.

Dauhajre, Andres, E. Riley, R. Mena, and J. A. Guerrero. 1989. *Impacto Economico de las Zonas Francas Industriales de Exportación en la Republica Dominicana.* Santo Domingo: Fundacion Economia y Desarrollo.

Deecke, H., T. Kruger, and D. Lapple. 1993. "Alternative Szenarien der wirtschaftlichen Strukturentwicklung in der Hamburger Wirtschaft unter raumlichen Gesichtspunkten." Final Report for the City of Hamburg. Hamburg: Technische Universität HamburgHarburg.

Deere, Carmen Diana, Peggy Antrobus, Lynn Bolles, Edwin Melendez, Peter Phillips, Marcia Rivera, and Helen Safa. 1990. *In the Shadows of the Sun: Caribbean Development Alternatives and U.S. Policy.* Boulder, CO: Westview.

Delauney, Jean Claude, and Jean Gadrey. 1987. *Les enjeux de la societe de service.* Paris: Presses de la Fondation des Sciences Politiques.

Dogan, M. and J. D. Kasarda, eds. 1988. *A World of Giant Cities.* Newbury Park, CA: Sage.

Dore, Ronald. 1986. *Flexible Rigidities: Industrial Policy and Structural Adjustment in the Japanese Economy, 1970-1980.* London: Athlone.

Drache, D. and M. Gertler, eds. 1991. *The New Era of Global Competition: State Policy and Market Power.* Montreal: McGill-Queen's University Press.

Drennan, Mathew P. 1989. "Information Intensive Industries in Metropolitan Areas of the United States." *Environment and Planning A* 21:1603-18.

————. 1992. "Gateway Cities: The Metropolitan Sources of U.S. Producer Service Exports." *Urban Studies* 29(2):217-35.

Duarte, R. 1989. "Heterogeneidade no Setor Informal: Um Estudo de Microunidades Produtivas em Aracaju e Teresina." *Estudios Economicos,* Fipe 19(Numero Especial):99-123.

duRivage, Virginia L., ed. 1992. *New Policies for the Part-Time and Contingent Workforce.* Washington, DC: Economic Policy Institute.

Eade, John. 1997. *Living the Global City: Globalization as a Local Process.* New York: Routledge.

Edel, Matthew. 1986. "Capitalism, Accumulation and the Explanation of Urban Phenomena." In *Urbanization and Urban Planning in Capitalist Society,* edited by Michael Dear and Allen Scott. New York: Methuen.

El-Shakhs, Salah. 1972. "Development, Primacy and Systems of Cities." *Journal of Developing Areas* 7(October):11-36.

Eurocities. 1989. *Documents and Subjects of Eurocities Conference.* Barcelona, April 21-22.

European Institute of Urban Affairs. 1992. *Urbanisation and the Functions of Cities in the European Community: A Report to the Commission of the European Communities, Directorate General for Regional Policy (XVI).* Liverpool: Liverpool John Moores University.

Fainstein, S. 1993. *The City Builders.* Oxford, UK: Blackwell.

Fainstein, S., N. Fainstein, R. C. Hill, D. R. Judd, and M. P. Smith. 1986. *Restructuring the City.* 2d ed. New York: Longman.

Fainstein, S., I. Gordon, and M. Harloe. 1992. *Divided Cities: Economic Restructuring and Social Change in London and New York.* New York: Blackwell.

Feldbauer, P., E. Pilz, D. Runzler, and I. Stacher, eds. 1993. *Megastädte: Zur Rolle von Metropolen in der Weltgesellschaft.* Vienna: Boehlau Verlag.

"Feminism and Globalization: The Impact of the Global Economy on Women and Feminist Theory." *Indiana Journal of Global Legal Studies* 4(1, Special issue).

Fernandez-Kelly, M. P. and A. M. Garcia. 1989. "Informalization at the Core: Hispanic Women, Homework, and the Advanced Capitalist State." In *The Informal Economy: Studies in Advanced and Less Developed Countries,* edited by A. Portes, M. Castells, and L. Benton. Baltimore: Johns Hopkins University Press.

Fernandez-Kelly, M. P. and Saskia Sassen. 1992. "Immigrant Women in the Garment and Electronic Industries in the New York-New Jersey Region and in Southern California." Final Research Report presented to the Ford, Revson, and Tinker Foundations, June, New York.

Figueroa, Janis Barry, Edwin Melendez, and Clara Rodriguez, eds. 1991. *Hispanics in the Labor Force.* New York: Plenum.

Friedmann, John. 1986. "The World City Hypothesis." *Development and Change* 17:69-84.

Friedmann, J. and G. Wolff. 1982. "World City Formation: An Agenda for Research and Action." *International Journal of Urban and Regional Research* 15(1):269-83.

"From Chatham House Man to Davos Man." 1997. *The Economist*, Febuary 1, Vol. 342, p. 18ff.

Frost, Martin and Nigel Spence. 1992. "Global City Characteristics and Central London's Employment." *Urban Studies* 30(3):547-58.

Fujita, Kuniko. 1991. "A World City and Flexible Specialization: Restructuring of the Tokyo Metropolis." *International Journal of Urban and Regional Research* 15(1):269-84.

Gad, Gunther. 1991. "Toronto's Financial District." *Canadian Urban Landscapes* 1:203-07.

Gans, Herbert. 1984. "American Urban Theory and Urban Areas." In *Cities in Recession*, edited by Ivan Szelenyi. Beverly Hills, CA: Sage.

Garofalo, G. and M. S. Fogarty. 1979. "Urban Income Distribution and the Urban Hierarchy-Inequality Hypothesis." *Review of Economics and Statistics* 61:381-88.

GaWC (Global Cities and World Cities Study Group and Network). 1998. http://www.lboro.ac.uk/departments/gy/research/gawc.html.

Gerlach, Michael. 1992. *Alliance Capitalism: The Social Organization of Japanese Business*. Berkeley: University of California Press.

Gershuny, Jonathan and Ian Miles. 1983. *The New Service Economy: The Transformation of Employment in Industrial Societies*. New York: Praeger.

Giarini, Orio, ed. 1987. *The Emerging Service Economy*. Oxford and New York: Pergamon.

Giddens, A. 1991. *The Consequences of Modernity*. Oxford, UK: Polity.

Gilbert, Allan, ed. 1996. *Cities in Latin America*. Tokyo: United Nations University Press.

Gillette, A. and A. Sayad. 1984. *L'immigration Algerienne en France*. 2d ed. Paris: Editions Entente.

Glickman, N. J. 1979. *The Growth and Management of the Japanese Urban System*. New York: Academic Press.

Glickman, N. J. and A. K. Glasmeier. 1989. "The International Economy and the American South." In *Deindustrialization and Regional Economic Transformation: The Experience of the United States*, edited by L. Rodwin and H. Sazanami. Winchester, MA: Unwin Hyman.

Glickman, N. J. and D. P. Woodward. 1989. *The New Competitors: How Foreign Investors Are Changing the U.S. Economy*. New York: Basic Books.

"Global City: Zitadellen der Internationalisierung." 1995. *Wissenschaft Forum* 12(2, Special Issue).

Goddard, J. B. 1993. "Information and Communications Technologies, Corporate Hierarchies and Urban Hierarchies in the New Europe." Presented at the Fourth International Workshop on Technological Change and Urban Form: Productive and Sustainable Cities, April 14-16, Berkeley, CA.

Goldsmith, William V. and Edward J. Blakely. 1992. *Separate Societies: Poverty and Inequality in U.S. Cities*. Philadelphia: Temple University Press.

Goldthorpe, John, ed. 1984. *Order and Conflict in Contemporary Capitalism.* Oxford. UK: Clarendon.

Gordon, Ian and Saskia Sassen. 1992. "Restructuring the Urban Labor Markets." Pp. 105-28 in *Divided Cities: New York and London in the Contemporary World,* edited by S. Fainstein, I. Gordon, and M. Harloe. Oxford, UK: Blackwell.

Graham, Edward M. and Paul R. Krugman. 1989. *Foreign Direct Investment in the United States.* Washington, DC: Institute for International Economics.

Graham, Stephen and Marvin, Simon. 1996. *Telecommunications and the City: Electronic Spaces, Urban Places.* London: Routledge.

Granovetter, Mark. 1985. "Economic Action and Social Structure: The Problem of Embeddedness." *American Journal of Sociology* 91:481-510.

Gravesteijn, S. G. E., S. van Griensven, and M. C. de Smidt, eds. 1998. "Timing Global Cities." *Nederlandse Geografische Studies* 241(Special issue).

Gregory, Derek and John Urry, eds. 1985. *Social Relations and Spatial Structures.* London: Macmillan.

Grosfoguel, Ramon. 1993. "Global Logics in the Caribbean City System: The Case of Miami and San Juan." In *World Cities in a World System,* edited by P. Knox and P. Taylor. New York: Cambridge University Press.

Grosz, E. 1992. "Bodies-Cities." Pp. 241-53 in *Sexuality & Space,* edited by Beatriz Colomina. Princeton Papers on Architecture. Princeton, NJ: Princeton Architectural Press.

Hall, Peter. 1964. *Greater London.* London: Faber & Faber.

———. 1966. *The World Cities.* New York: McGraw-Hill.

———. 1988. *Cities of Tomorrow.* Oxford, UK: Blackwell.

Hall, P. and D. Hay. 1980. *Growth Centers in the European Urban System.* London: Heinemann Educational Books.

Hall, Rodney Bruce. *National Collective Identity.* 1999. New York: Columbia University Press.

Hall, S. 1991. "The Local and the Global: Globalization and Ethnicity." In *Current Debates in Art History 3. Culture, Globalization and the World-System: Contemporary Conditions for the Representation of Identity,* edited by Anthony D. King. New York: State University of New York at Binghamton, Department of Art and Art History.

Hardoy, J. E. 1975. *Urbanization in Latin America.* Garden City, NJ: Anchor.

Hardoy, J. E. and D. Satterthwaite. 1989. *Squatter Citizen: Life in the Urban Third World.* London: Earthscan.

Harris, R. 1991. "The Geography of Employment and Residence in New York Since 1950." Pp. 129-52 in *Dual City: Restructuring New York,* edited by J. Mollenkopf and M. Castells. New York: Russell Sage.

Harrison, B. and B. Bluestone. 1988. *The Great U-Turn.* New York: Basic Books.

Hartmann, Heidi, ed. 1987. *Computer Chips and Paper Clips: Technology and Women's Employment.* Washington, DC: National Academy Press.

Harvey, David. 1985. *The Urbanization of Capital.* Oxford, UK: Blackwell.

————. 1989. *The Condition of Postmodernity*. Oxford, UK: Blackwell.

Hausserman, Hartmut and Walter Siebel. 1987. *Neue Urbanität*. Frankfurt: Suhrkamp Verlag.

Henderson, Jeff and Manuel Castells, eds. 1987. *Global Restructuring and Territorial Development*. London: Sage.

Hill, R. C. 1989. "Comparing Transnational Production Systems: The Case of the Automobile Industry in the United States and Japan." *International Journal of Urban and Regional Research* 13(3):462.

Hino, Masateru. 1984. "The Location of Head and Branch Offices of Large Enterprises in Japan." *Science Reports of Tohoku University* (Senday, Japan), Geography Series 34(2):**000-000**.

Hirst, Paul and Jonathan Zeitlin. 1989. *Reversing Industrial Decline?* Oxford, UK: Berg.

Hitz, Keil, Lehrer, Ronneberger, Schmid, and Wolff, eds. 1995. *Capitales Fatales*. Zurich: Rotpunkt Publishers.

Hollifield, James F. 1992. *Immigrants, Markets, and States: The Political Economy of Postwar Europe*. Cambridge, MA: Harvard University Press.

Hoover's Handbook of World Business. 1998. Austin, TX: Reference Press.

Hymer, Stephen and Robert Rowthorn. 1970. "Multinational Corporations and International Oligopoly." In *The International Corporation*, edited by Charles P. Kindleberger. Cambridge: MIT Press.

IMF (International Money Fund). *International Capital Markets Report*. Washington, DC: IMF.

Inda, Jonathan Xavier, Louis F. Miron, and Rodolfo D. Torres. 1999. *Race, Identity, and Citizenship*. Oxford, UK: Blackwell.

Ishizuka, H. and Y. Ishida. 1988. *Tokyo: Urban Growth and Planning, 1968-1988*. Tokyo: Tokyo Metropolitan University, Center for Urban Studies.

Ito, Tatsuo and Masafumi Tanifuji. 1982. "The Role of Small and Intermediate Cities in National Development in Japan." In *Small Cities and National Development*, edited by O. P. Mathur. Nagoya, Japan: U.N. Centre for Regional Development.

Iyotani, Toshio. 1989. "The New Immigrant Workers in Tokyo." Typescript, Tokyo University of Foreign Studies.

Iyotani, Toshio and Toshio Naito. 1989. "Tokyo no Kokusaika de Tenkan Semarareru Chusho Kigyo" [Medium- and small-sized corporations under pressure of change by Tokyo's internationalization]. *Ekonomisuto*, September 5, pp. 44-49.

Japan Ministry of Labor. Various years. *Monthly Labor Statistics and Research Bulletin*. Tokyo: Ministry of Labor.

Jenkins, Rhys. 1991. "The Political Economy of Industrialization: A Comparison of Latin American and East Asian Newly Industrializing Countries." *Development and Change* 11:197-231.

Jessop, Robert. 1999. "Reflections on Globalization and Its Illogics." Pp. 19-38 in *Globalization and the Asian Pacific: Contested Territories*, edited by Kris

Olds, Peter Dicken, Philip F. Kelly, Lilly Kong, and Henry Wai-Chung Yeung. London: Routledge.

Jonas, S. 1992. *The Battle for Guatemala: Rebels, Death Squads, and U.S. Power.* Boulder, CO: Westview.

Kahnert, Friedrich. 1987. "Improving Urban Employment and Labor Productivity." World Bank Discussion paper No. 10. Washington, DC: World Bank.

Kasarda, John D. and Edward M. Crenshaw. 1991. "Third World Urbanization: Dimensions, Theories and Determinants." *Annual Review of Sociology* 17:467-501.

Kasinitz, Philip. 1992. *Caribbean New York.* Ithaca, NY: Cornell University Press.

Keil, Roger and Klaus Ronneberger. 1992. "Going up the Country: Internationalization and Urbanization on Frankfurt's Northern Fringe." Presented at the UCLA International Sociological Association, Research Committee 29, *A New Urban and Regional Hierarchy? Impacts of Modernization, Restructuring and the End of Bipolarity,* April 24-26, Los Angeles, CA.

————. 1995. "The City Turned Inside Out: Spatial Strategies and Local Politics." In *Capitales Fatales,* edited by H. Hitz, R. Keil, V. Lehrer, K. Ronneberger, C. Schmid, and R. Wolff. Zurich: Rotpunkt Publishers.

Kelly, Maryellen R. 1989. "Alternative Forms of Work Organization under Programmable Automation." Pp. 235-46 in *The Transformation of Work?* edited by Stephen Wood. London: Unwin-Hyman.

King, A. D. 1990. *Urbanism, Colonialism, and the World Economy. Culture and Spatial Foundations of the World Urban System.* International Library of Sociology. London and New York: Routledge.

————, ed. 1996. *Re-presenting the City. Ethnicity, Capital and Culture in the 21st Century.* London: Macmillan.

Klopp, Brett. 1998. "Integration and Political Representation in a Multicultural City: The Case of Frankfurt am Main." *German Politics and Society* 16(4):42-68.

Knight, R. V. and G. Gappert, eds. 1989. *Cities in a Global Society.* Vol. 35. Urban Affairs Annual Reviews. Newbury Park, CA: Sage.

Knox, P. and P. Taylor, eds. 1995. *World Cities in a World-System.* New York: Cambridge University Press.

Komai, Hiroshi. 1992. "Are Foreign Trainees in Japan Disguised Cheap Laborers?" *Migration World* 10(1):13-17.

Komlosy, A., C. Parnreiter, I. Stacher, and S. Zimmerman, eds. 1997. *Ungeregelt und Unterbezahlt: Der Informelle Sektor in der Weltwirtschaft.* Frankfurt: Brandes & Apsel/Sudwind.

Komori, S. 1983. "Inner City in Japanese Context." *City Planning Review* 125:11-17.

Kowarick, L., A. M. Campos, and M. C. de Mello. 1991. "Os Percursos de Desigualdade." In *São Paulo, Crise e Mudanca,* edited by R. Rolnik, L. Kowarick, and N. Somekh. São Paulo: Brasiliense.

Kunzmann, K. R. and M. Wegener. 1991. "The Pattern of Urbanisation in Western Europe 1960-1990." Report for the Directorate General XVI of the Commission of the European Communities as part of the study *Urbanisation and the Function of Cities in the European Community*. Dortmund, Germany: Institut für Raumplanung.

KUPI (Kobe Urban Problems Institute). 1981. *Policy for Revitalization of Inner City*. Kobe: KUPI.

Kuttner, Robert. 1991. *The End of Laissez-Faire*. New York: Knopf.

Landell-Mills, Pierre, Ramgopal Agarwala, and Stanley Please. 1989. *Sub-Saharan Africa: From Crisis to Sustainable Growth*. Washington, DC: World Bank.

Lash, Scott and John Urry. 1987. *The End of Organized Capitalism*. Cambridge, UK: Polity.

———. 1994. *Economies of Signs and Space*. London: Sage.

Lavinas, Lena and Maria Regina Nabuco. 1992. "Economic Crisis and Flexibility in Brazilian Labor Markets." Presented at the UCLA International Sociological Association, Research Committee 29, *A New Urban and Regional Hierarchy? Impacts of Modernization, Restructuring and the End of Bipolarity*, April 24-26, Los Angeles, CA.

Leborgne, D. and A. Lipietz. 1988. "L'après-Fordisme et son espace." *Les Temps Modernes* 43:75-114.

Lee, Kyu Sik. 1989. *The Location of Jobs in a Developing Metropolis: Patterns of Growth in Bogota and Cali, Colombia*. New York: Oxford University Press.

LeGates, R. T. and F. Stout, eds. 1996. *The City Reader*. New York: Routledge.

Levine, Marc V. 1990. *The Reconquest of Montreal: Language Policy and Social Change in a Bilingual City*. Philadelphia: Temple University Press.

Levy, Frank and Richard Murname. 1992. "U.S. Earnings Levels and Earnings Inequality: A Review of Recent Trends and Proposed Explanations." *Journal of Economic Literature* (September):1333-81.

Leyshon, A., P. Daniels, and N. Thrift. 1987. "Large Accountancy Firms in the U.K.: Spatial Development." Working Paper, St. David's University College, Lampeter, U.K., and University of Liverpool.

Light, I. and E. Bonacich. 1988. *Immigrant Enterprise*. Berkeley: University of California Press.

Linn, Johannes F. 1983. *Cities in the Developing World: Policies for Their Equitable and Efficient Growth*. New York and Oxford: Oxford University Press.

Lipietz, A. 1988. "New Tendencies in the International Division of Labor: Regimes of Accumulation and Modes of Regulation." In *Production, Work, Territory*, edited by A. Scott and M. Storper. Boston: Allen & Unwin.

Lo, Fu-chen and Y. Yeung, eds. 1996. *Emerging World Cities in Pacific Asia*. Tokyo: United Nations University Press.

Logan, J. R. and H. Molotch. 1987. *Urban Fortunes*. Berkeley: University of California Press.

Logan, J. R. and T. Swanstrom, eds. 1990. *Beyond the City Limits: Urban Policy and Economic Restructuring in Comparative Perspective.* Philadelphia: Temple University Press.

Lomnitz, Larissa. 1985. "Mechanisms of Articulation between Shantytown Settlers and the Urban System." *Urban Anthropology* 7:185-205.

Lozano, Beverly. 1989. *The Invisible Work Force: Transforming American Business with Outside and Home-Based Workers.* New York: Free Press.

Lozano, Wilfredo and Isis Duarte. 1991. "Proceso de Urbanización, Modelos de Desarrollo y Clases Sociales en Republica Dominicana: 1960-1990." Paper presented at the seminar on Urbanization in the Caribbean in the Years of Crisis, May 29-June 1, Florida International University, Miami.

Machimura, Takashi. 1992. "The Urban Restructuring Process in the 1980s: Transforming Tokyo into a World City" *International Journal of Urban and Regional Research* 16(1):114-28.

Marcuse, Peter. 1986. "Abandonment, Gentrification, and Displacement: The Linkages in New York City." In *Gentrification of the City*, edited by Neil Smith and Peter Williams. Boston: Allen & Unwin.

Marie, Claude-Valentin. 1992. "Les etrangers non-salaries en France, symbole de la mutation economique des années 80." *Revue Européenne des Migrations Internationales* 8(10):27-38.

Markusen, A. 1985. *Profit Cycles, Oligopoly, and Regional Development.* Cambridge: MIT Press.

Markusen, A. and V. Gwiasda. 1991. "Multipolarity and the Layering of Functions in the World Cities: New York City's Struggle to Stay on Top." Presented at the Conference *New York, Tokyo and Paris*, October, Tokyo.

Markusen, A., P. Hall, S. Campbell, and S. Deitrick, eds. 1991. *The Rise of the Gunbelt.* New York: Oxford University Press.

Markusen, A., P. Hall, and A. Glasmeier. 1986. *High Tech America: The What, How, Where and Why of the Sunrise Industries.* London/Boston: Allen & Unwin.

Marlin, John Tepper, Immanuel Ness, and Stephen T. Collins. 1986. *Book of World City Rankings.* New York: Macmillan.

Marshall, J. N. et al. 1986. "Uneven Development in the Service Economy: Understanding the Location and Role of Producer Services." Report of the Producer Services Working Party, Institute of British Geographers and the ESRC, August.

Martinelli, Flavia and Erica Schoenberger. 1991. "Oligopoly Is Alive and Well: Notes for a Broader Discussion of Flexible Accumulation." In *Industrial Change and Regional Development: The Transformation of New Industrial Spaces,* edited by Georges Benko and Mick Dunford. London and New York: Belhaven/Pinter.

Masser, I., O. Sviden, and M. Wegener. 1990. "Europe 2020: Long-Term Scenarios of Transport and Communications in Europe." Unpublished paper for the European Science Foundation.

Massey, Doreen. 1984. *Spatial Divisions of Labour: Social Structures and the Geography of Production.* London: Macmillan.

Massey, Douglas S. and Nancy Denton. 1998. *American Apartheid: Segregation and the Making of the Underclass.* Cambridge, MA: Harvard University Press.

Mayer, Margit. "Shifts in the Local Political System in European Cities since the 80s." In *Competition, Regulation and the New Europe,* edited by Mick Dunford and Grigoris Kafkalas. London: Belhaven.

McDowell, Linda. 1997. *Capital Culture.* Oxford, UK: Blackwell.

Melendez, E., C. Rodriguez, and J. B. Figueroa. 1991. *Hispanics in the Labor Force.* New York: Plenum.

Meridian Securities Markets. 1998. *World Stock Exchange Fact Book.* Morris Plains, NJ: Electronic Commerce.

Meyer, David R. 1991. "Change in the World System of Metropolises: The Role of Business Intermediaries." *Urban Geography* 12(5):393-416.

Meyer, John R. and James M. Gustafson, eds. 1988. *The U.S. Business Corporation: An Institution in Transition.* Cambridge, MA: Ballinger.

Mignaqui, Iliana. 1998. "Dinamica Immobiliaria y Transformaciones Metropolitanas." In *Ciudades y Regiones al Avance de la Globalización,* edited by S. Sorenstein and R. Bustos Cara. UNS (Universidad Nacional del Sur), Bahia Blanca:255-84.

Mingione, E. 1991. *Fragmented Societies: A Sociology of Economic Life beyond the Market Paradigm.* Oxford, UK: Blackwell.

Mingione, E. and E. Pugliese. 1988. "La Questione Urbana e Rurale: Tra Superamento Teorico e Problemi di Confini Incerti." *La Critica Sociologica* 85:17-50.

Mioni, Alberto. 1991. "Legittimita ed Efficacia del Progetto Urbano." *Dis T Rassegna di Studi e Ricerche del Dipartimento di Scienze del Territorio del Politecnico di Milano* 9(September):137-50.

Mitter, S., ed. 1989. *Information Technology and Women's Employment: The Case of the European Clothing Industry.* Berlin and New York: Springer Verlag.

Miyajima, Takashi. 1989. *The Logic of Receiving Foreign Workers: Among Dilemmas of Advanced Societies* (Gaikokujin Rodosha Mukaeire no Ronri: Senshin shakai no Jirenma no naka de). Tokyo: Akashi Shoten.

Montgomery, Cynthia A. and Michael E. Porter, eds. 1991. *Strategy: Seeking and Securing Competitive Advantage.* Boston: Harvard Business School Press.

Morita, Kiriro. 1990. "Japan and the Problem of Foreign Workers." Research Institute for the Japanese Economy, Faculty of Economics, University of Tokyo-Hongo.

———. 1993. "Foreign Workers." Unpublished paper, Department of Economics, University of Tokyo.

Morita, Kiriro and Saskia Sassen. 1994. "The New Illegal Immigration in Japan, 1980-1992." *International Migration Review* 28(1):153.

Morris, M. 1992. "Great Moments in Social Climbing: King Kong and the Human Fly." In *Sexuality and Space*, edited by Beatriz Colomina. Princeton Papers on Architecture. Princeton, NJ: Princeton Architectural Press.

Mowery, David, ed. 1988. *International Collaborative Ventures in U.S. Manufacturing*. Cambridge, MA: Ballinger.

Nabuco, M. R., A. F. Machado, and J. Pires. 1991. *Estrategias de Vida e Sobrevivencia na Industria de Confeccoes de Belo Horizonte*. Belo Horizonte, Brazil: Cedeplar/UFMG.

Nakabayashi, Itsuki. 1987. "Social-Economic and Living Conditions of Tokyo's Inner City." *Geographical Reports of Tokyo Metropolitan University* 22.

Nanami, Tadashi and Yasuo Kuwabara, eds. 1989. *Tomorrow's Neighbors: Foreign Workers* (Asu no Rinjin: Gaikokujin Rodosha). Tokyo: Toyo Keizai Shimposha.

Nelson, J. I. and J. Lorence. 1985. "Employment in Service Activities and Inequality in Metropolitan Areas." *Urban Affairs Quarterly* 21(1):106-25.

Noyelle, T. and A. B. Dutka. 1988. *International Trade in Business Services: Accounting, Advertising, Law and Management Consulting*. Cambridge, MA: Ballinger.

O'Connor, K. 1990. *State of Australia*. Clayton: National Centre for Australian Studies, Monash University.

Olds, Kris, Peter Dicken, Philip F. Kelly, Lilly Kong, and Henry Wai-Chung Yeung, eds. 1999. *Globalizatioon and the Asian Pacific: Contested Territories*. London: Routledge.

Oliver, Nick and Barry Wilkinson. 1988. *The Japanization of British Industry*. Oxford, UK: Blackwell.

Ong, Aihwa and Donald Nonini, eds. 1997. *Underground Empires*. New York: Routledge.

Palumbo-Liu, David. 1999. *Asian/American*. Stanford, CA: Stanford University Press.

Parkinson, M., B. Foley, and D. R. Judd, eds. 1989. *Regenerating the Cities: The U.K. Crisis and the U.S. Experience*. Glenview, IL: Scott Foresman.

Peraldi, M. and E. Perrin, eds. 1996. *Reseaux productifs et territoires urbains*. Toulouse: Presses Universitaires de Mirail.

Perez-Sainz, J. P. 1992. *Informalidad Urbana en America Latina: Enfoques, Problematicas e Interrogantes*. Caracas, Venezuela: Editorial Nueva Sociedad.

Perez-Stable, Marifeli and Miren Uriarte. 1993. "Cubans and the Changing Economy of Miami." Pp. 133-59 in *Latinos in a Changing U.S. Economy: Comparative Perspectives on Growing Inequality*, edited by Rebecca Morales and Frank Bonilla. Sage Series on Race and Ethnic Relations, Vol. 7. Newbury Park, CA: Sage.

Petrella, R. 1990. "Technology and the Firm." *Technology Analysis & Strategic Management* 2:2.

Pickvance, C. and E. Preteceille, eds. 1991. *State Restructuring and Local Power: A Comparative Perspective.* London: Pinter.

Polanyi, Karl. 1975. *The Great Transformation: The Political and Economic Origins of Our Time.* Boston: Beacon.

Portes, A., M. Castells, and L. Benton, eds. 1989. *The Informal Economy: Studies in Advanced and Less Developed Countries.* Baltimore: Johns Hopkins University Press.

Portes, A. and M. Lungo, eds. 1992a. *Urbanización en Centroamerica.* San José, Costa Rica: Facultad Latinoamericana de Ciencias Sociales.

―――, eds. 1992b. *Urbanización en el Caribe.* San José, Costa Rica: Facultad Latinoamericana de Ciencias Sociales.

Portes, A. and S. Sassen-Koob. 1987. "Making It Underground: Comparative Material on the Informal Sector in Western Market Economies." *American Journal of Sociology* 93:30-61.

Portes, Alejandro and Alex Stepick. 1993. *City on the Edge: The Transformation of Miami.* Berkeley: University of California Press.

Portes, Alejandro and Min Zhou. 1992. "Gaining the Upper Hand: Economic Mobility among Immigrant and Domestic Minorities." *Ethnic and Racial Studies* 15(October):492-522.

Powell, Walter. 1990. "Neither Market nor Hierarchy: Network Forms of Organization." In *Research in Organizational Behavior,* edited by Barry M. Straw and Larry L. Cummings. Greenwich, CT: JAI.

Pozos Ponce, Fernando. 1996. *Metropolis en Reestructuración: Guadalajara y Monterrey 1980-1989.* Guadalajara, Mexico: Universidad de Guadalajara, con apoyo de El Fondo para la Modernización de la Educación Superior.

Prader, T., ed. 1992. *Moderne Sklaven: Asyl und Migrationspolitik in Österreich.* Vienna: Promedia.

PREALC. (1982). *Mercado de Trabajo en Cifras: 1950-1080.* Santiago de Chile: International Labour Office.

―――. 1987. *Ajuste y Deuda Social: Un Enfoque Estructural.* Santiago de Chile: International Labour Office.

Preteceille, E. 1986. "Collective Consumption, Urban Segregation, and Social Classes." *Environment and Planning D: Society and Space* 4:145-54.

Prigge, Walter. 1991. "Zweite Moderne: Modernisierung und Städtische Kultur in Frankfurt." Pp. 97-105 in *Frankfurt am Main: Stadt, Soziologie und Kultur,* edited by Frank-Olaf Brauerhoch. Frankfurt: Vervuert.

Pugliese, E. 1983. "Aspetti dell' Economia Informale a Napoli." *Inchiesta* 13(59-60):89-97.

Queiroz Ribeiro, Luis Cesar de. 1990. "Restructuring in Large Brazilian Cities: The Center/Periphery Model in Question." Research Institute of Urban and Regional Planning, Federal University of Rio de Janeiro.

Rakatansky, M. 1992. "Spatial Narratives." Pp. 198-221 in *Strategies in Architectural Thinking,* edited by J. Whiteman, J. Kipnis, and R. Burdett. Chicago/

Cambridge, MA: Chicago Institute for Architecture and Urbanism/MIT Press.

Ramirez, Nelson, Isidor Santana, Francisco de Moya, and Pablo Tactuk. 1988. *Republica Dominicana: Población y Desarrollo 1950-1985.* San José, Costa Rica: Centro Latinoamericano de Demografia (CELADE).

RECLUS. 1989. *Les villes européennes.* Rapport pour la DATAR. Paris: RECLUS.

Regional Employment Program for Latin America and the Caribbean (PREALC). 1982. *Mercado de Trabajo en Cifras: 1950-1980.* Santiago de Chile: International Labour Office.

Reich, Robert B. 1991. *The Work of Nations: Preparing Ourselves for 21st Century Capitalism.* New York: Knopf.

Renooy, P. H. 1984. "Twilight Economy: A Survey of the Informal Economy in the Netherlands." Research Report, Faculty of Economic Sciences, University of Amsterdam.

Rimmer, P. J. 1986. "Japan's World Cities: Tokyo, Osaka, Nagoya or Tokaido Megalopolis?" *Development and Change* 17(1):121-58.

———. 1988. "Japanese Construction and the Australian States: Another Round of Interstate Rivalry." *International Journal of Urban and Regional Research* 12(3):404-24.

Roberts, B. 1973. *Organizing Strangers: Poor Families in Guatemala City.* Austin: University of Texas Press.

Roberts, B. 1976. *Cities of Peasants.* London: Edward Arnold.

———. *The Making of Citizens: Cities of Peasants Revisited.* New York: Edward Arnold.

Roberts, Susan. 1994. "Fictitious Capital, Fictitious Spaces: The Geography of Off-shore Financial Flows." In *Money, Power and Space,* edited by S. Corbridge, R. Martin, and N. Thrift. Oxford, UK: Blackwell.

Rodriguez, Nestor P. and J. R. Feagin. 1986. "Urban Specialization in the World System." *Urban Affairs Quarterly* 22(2):187-220.

Rolnik, R., L. Kowarick, and N. Somekh, eds. 1991. *São Paulo Crise e Mudanca.* São Paulo, Brazil: Brasiliense.

Roncayolo, M. 1990. *L'imaginaire de Marseille.* Marseille: Chambre de Commerce et d'Industrie de Marseille.

Rosen, F. and D. McFadyen, eds. 1995. *Free Trade and Economic Restructuring in Latin America* (NACLA reader). New York: Monthly Review Press.

Ross, R. and K. Trachte. 1983. "Global Cities and Global Classes: The Peripheralization of Labor in New York City." *Review* 6(3):393-431.

Rotzer, Florian. 1995. *Die Telepolis: Urbanität im Digitalen Zeitalter.* Mannheim, Germany: Bollman.

Roulleau-Berger, Laurence. 1999. *Le travail en friche.* La Tour d'Aigues: Editions de l'Aube.

Roy, Olivier. 1991. "Ethnicité, bandes et communautarisme." *Esprit* (February):37-47.

Sachar, A. 1990. "The Global Economy and World Cities." Pp. 149-60 in *The World Economy and the Spatial Organization of Power*, edited by A. Sachar and S. Oberg. Aldershot, UK: Avebury.

Salzinger, Leslie. 1995. "A Maid by Any Other Name: The Transformation of 'Dirty Work' by Central American Immigrants." Pp. 139-60 in *Ethnography Unbound: Power and Resistance in the Modern Metropolis*, edited by Michael Burawoy. Berkeley: University of California Press.

Sanchez, Roberto and Tito Alegria. 1992. "Las Cuidades de la Frontera Norte." Departamento de Estudios Urbanos y Medio Ambiente, El Colegio de la Frontera Norte, Tijuana, Mexico.

Santos, Milton, Maria Adelia A. De Souze, and Maria Laura Silveira, eds. 1994. *Territorio Globalizacao e Fragmentacao*. São Paulo, Brazil: Hucitec.

Santoso, Oerip Lestari Djoko. 1992. "The Role of Surakarta Area in the Industrial Transformation and Development of Central Java." *Regional Development Dialogue* 13(2):69-82.

Saskai, Nobuo. 1991. *Tocho: Mo Hitotsu no Seifu* (The Tokyo Metropolitan Government: Another Central Government). Tokyo: Iwanami Shoten.

Sassen, Saskia. 1988. *The Mobility of Labor and Capital: A Study in International Investment and Labor Flow*. New York: Cambridge University Press.

———. 1991. *The Global City: New York, London, Tokyo*. Princeton, NJ: Princeton University Press.

———. 1996. *Losing Control? Sovereignty in an Age of Globalization*. The 1995 Columbia University Leonard Hastings Schoff Memorial Lectures. New York: Columbia University Press.

———. 1998. *Globalization and Its Discontents: Selected Essays*. New York: New Press.

———. 1999. "Global Financial Centers." *Foreign Affairs* 78(1):75-87.

———. , ed. 2000. *Cities and Their Crossborder Networks*. Tokyo: United Nations.

Sassen-Koob, Saskia. 1980. "Immigrants and Minority Workers in the Organization of the Labor Process." *Journal of Ethnic Studies* 8(Spring):1-34.

———. 1982. "Recomposition and Peripheralization at the Core." Pp. 88-100 *Immigration and Change in the International Division of Labor*. San Francisco: Synthesis. (Reprinted in *Contemporary Marxism*, Vol. 4.)

———. 1984. "The New Labor Demand in Global Cities." Pp. 139-71 in *Cities in Transformation*, edited by M. P. Smith. Beverly Hills, CA: Sage.

Savitch, H. 1988. *Post-Industrial Cities*. Princeton, NJ: Princeton University Press.

———. 1996. "Cities in a Global Era: A New Paradigm for the Next Millenium." Pp. 39-65 in *Preparing for the Urban Future: Global Pressures and Local Forces*, edited by M. Cohen, B. Ruble, J. Tulchin, and A. Garland. Washington, DC: Woodrow Wilson Center Press (Distributed by Johns Hopkins University Press).

Sayer, Andrew and Richard Walker. 1992. *The New Social Economy: Reworking the Division of Labor.* Cambridge, MA: Blackwell.

Schiffer, Sueli Ramos. 2000. "São Paulo: The Challenge of Globalization in an Exclusionary Urban Structure." In *Cities and Their Crossborder Networks,* edited by Saskia Sassen. Tokyo: United Nations University Press.

Sclar, Elliott D. and Walter Hook. 1993. "The Importance of Cities to the National Economy." In *Interwoven Destinies: Cities and the Nation,* edited by Henry G. Cisneros. New York: Norton.

Scott, Allen J. 1988. *Metropolis: From the Division of Labor to Urban Form.* Berkeley: University of California Press.

Scott, Allen J. and Michael Storper, eds. 1986. *Production, Work, Territory.* Boston: Allen & Unwin.

Sennett, R. 1990. *The Conscience of the Eye: The Design and Social Life of Cities.* New York: Knopf.

Sennett, R. 1998. *The Corrosion of Character: The Personal Consequences of Work in the New Capitalism.* New York: Norton.

"The Service 500." *Fortune,* May 31, 1993, pp. 199-230.

Shank, G., ed. 1994. "Japan Enters the 21st Century." *Social Justice* 21(2, Special issue).

Sheets, R. G., S. Nord, and J. J. Phelps. 1987. *The Impact of Service Industries on Underemployment in Metropolitan Economies.* Lexington, MA: D. C. Heath.

Short, J. R. and Y. H. Kim. 1999. *Globalization and the City.* New York: Longman.

Siebel, W. 1984. "Krisenphänomene der Stadtentwicklung." *arch + d* 75/76:67-70.

Silver, H. 1984. "Regional Shifts, Deindustrialization and Metropolitan Income Inequality." Presented at the Annual Meeting of the American Sociological Association, August, San Antonio, TX.

Simon, David. 1995. "The World City Hypothesis: Reflections from the Periphery." Pp. 132-55 in *World Cities in a World-System,* edited by P. Knox and P. Taylor. New York: Cambridge University Press.

Singelmann, J. 1974. "The Sectoral Transformation of the Labor Force in Seven Industrialized Countries, 1920-1960." Ph.D. dissertation, University of Texas, Austin.

Singelmann, J. and H. L. Browning. 1980. "Industrial Transformation and Occupational Change in the U.S., 1960-70." *Social Forces* 59:246-64.

Singh, Surjit. 1994. *Urban Informal Sector.* Jaipur: Rawat.

Sklair, Leslie. 1985. "Shenzhen: A Chinese 'Development Zone' in Global Perspective." *Development and Change, 16,* 571-602.

———. 1991. *Sociology of the Global System: Social Changes in Global Perspective.* Baltimore: Johns Hopkins University Press.

Smith, Carol A. 1985. "Theories and Measures of Urban Primacy: A Critique." In *Urbanization in the World-Economy,* edited by M. Timberlake. Orlando, FL: Academic Press.

Smith, David, ed. 1992. *The Apartheid City and Beyond: Urbanization and Social Change in South Africa.* London: Routledge/Witwatersrand University Press.

Smith, David, D. Solinger, and S. Topik, eds. 1999. *States and Sovereignty in the Global Economy.* London: Routledge.

Smith, David A. 1995. "The New Urban Sociology Meets the Old: Rereading Some Classical Human Ecology." *Urban Affairs Review* 30(3):432-57.

Smith, M. P. and J. R. Feagin. 1987. *The Capitalist City: Global Restructuring and Territorial Development.* London: Sage.

Smith, N. and P. Williams. 1986. *Gentrification of the City.* Boston: Allen & Unwin.

Smith, Robert C. 1997. "Transnational Migration, Assimilation, and Political Community." In *The City and the World,* edited by Margaret Crahan and Alberto Vourvoulias-Bush. New York: Council of Foreign Relations.

Solinger, Dorothy. 1999. *Contesting Citizenship in Urban China: Peasant Migrants, the State, and the Logic of the Market.* Berkeley: University of California Press.

Sonobe, M. 1993. "Spatial Dimension of Social Segregation in Tokyo: Some Remarks in Comparison with London." Paper presented at the meeting of the Global City Project, Social Science Research Council, March 9-11, New York.

SOPEMI (Systeme d'observation permanente pour les migrations). 1999. *Annual Report.* Paris: OECD, Directorate for Social Affairs, Manpower and Education.

Stanback, T. M., Jr., P. J. Bearse, T. J. Noyelle, and R. Karasek. 1981. *Services: The New Economy.* Montclair, NJ: Allenheld, Osmun.

Stanback, T. M. and T. J. Noyelle. 1982. *Cities in Transition: Changing Job Structures in Atlanta, Denver, Buffalo, Phoenix, Columbus (Ohio), Nashville, Charlotte.* Montclair, NJ: Allenheld, Osmun.

Stimson, Robert J. 1993. "The Process of Globalisation and Economic Restructuring and the Emergence of a New Space Economy of Cities and Regions in Australia." Presented at the Fourth International Workshop on Technological Change and Urban Form: Productive and Sustainable Cities, April 14-16, Berkeley, CA.

Stopford, John M., ed. 1992. *Directory of Multinationals.* London: Macmillan.

Stren, R. E. and R. R. White. 1989. *African Cities in Crisis: Managing Rapid Urban Growth.* Boulder, CO: Westview.

Susser, Ida. 1982. *Norman Street, Poverty and Politics in an Urban Neighborhood.* New York: Oxford University Press.

Tabak, Faruk. Forthcoming. *Informalization: Process and Structure.* Baltimore: Johns Hopkins University Press.

Taylor, P. J., D. R. F. Walker, and J. V. Beaverstock. 2000. "Introducing GaWC: Research World City Network Formation." In *Cities and Their Crossborder Networks,* edited by S. Sassen. Tokyo: United Nations University Press.

Teresaka, Akinobu et al. 1988. "The Transformation of Regional Systems in an Information-Oriented Society." *Geographical Review of Japan* 61(1):159-73.

Thomas, Margaret. 1983. "The Leading Euromarket Law Firms in Hong Kong and Singapore." *International Financial Law Review* (June):4-8.

Thomson Financial. 1999. *International Target Cities Report.* New York: Thomson Financial Investor Relations.

Thrift, N. 1987. "The Fixers: The Urban Geography of International Commercial Capital." In *Global Restructuring and Territorial Development,* edited by J. Henderson and M. Castells. London: Sage.

Todd, Graham. 1993. "The Political Economy of Urban and Regional Restructuring in Canada: Toronto, Montreal and Vancouver in the Global Economy, 1970-1990." Ph.D. dissertation, Department of Political Science, York University, Toronto, Canada.

———. 1995. " 'Going Global' in the Semi-periphery: World Cities as Political Projects. The Case of Toronto." Pp. 192-214 in *World Cities in a World-System,* edited by P. Knox and P. Taylor. New York: Cambridge University Press.

Toulouse, Christopher. 1992. "Thatcherism, Class Politics and Urban Development in London." *Critical Sociology* 18(1):57-76.

Timberlake, M., ed. 1985. *Urbanization in the World Economy.* Orlando, FL: Academic Press.

Trejos, J. D. 1991. "Informalidad y Acumulación en el Area Metropolitana de San José, Costa Rica." In *Informalidad Urbana en Centroamerica: Entre la Acumulación y la Subsistencia,* edited by J. P. Perez-Sainz and R. Menjivar Larin. Caracas, Venezuela: Editorial Nueva Sociedad.

Tribalat, M., J.-P. Garson, Y. Moulier-Boutang, and R. Silberman. 1991. *Cent Ans d'immigration: Etrangers d'hier, français d'aujourd'hui.* Paris: Presses Universitaires de France, Institut National d'Etudes Demographiques.

United Nations. 1992. *World Investment Report 1992: Transnational Corporations as Engines of Growth.* New York: United Nations.

U.N. Center on Transnational Corporations (UNCTC). 1991. *World Investment Report: The Triad in Foreign Direct Investment.* New York: United Nations.

———. 1992. *The Determinants of Foreign Direct Investment: A Survey of the Evidence.* New York: United Nations.

U.N. Conference on Trade and Development (UNCTAD), Programme on Transnational Corporations. 1993. *World Investment Report 1993: Transnational Corporations and Integrated International Production.* New York: United Nations.

———. 1997. *World Investment Report 1997: Transnational Corporations, Market Structure and Competition Policy.* New York: United Nations.

———. 1998. *World Investment Report 1998: Trends and Determinants.* New York: United Nations.

U.N. Department for International Economic and Social Affairs. 1987. *Prospects of World Urbanization.* New York: United Nations.

U.N. Department for Economic and Social Affairs, Policy Analysis. 1994. *Urban Agglomerations and Rural Agglomerations, 1994.* New York: United Nations.

U.N. Department of Economic and Social Affairs, Population Division. 1996. *Urban Agglomerations, 1996.* New York: United Nations.

U.S. Bureau of Labor. 1998. *U.S. Bureau of Labor Statistics Data.* Washington, DC: Government Printing Office.

U.S. Bureau of the Census. 1997. *U.S. Census Update.* Washington, DC: Government Printing Office.

U.S. Department of Commerce, Office of the U.S. Trade Representative. 1983. *U.S. National Study on Trade in Services.* Washington, DC: Government Printing Office.

U.S. Department of Commerce. 1985. *U.S. Direct Investment Abroad: 1982 Benchmark Survey Data.* Washington, DC: Government Printing Office.

———. 1992. *U.S. Direct Investment Abroad: 1989 Benchmark Survey, Final Results.* Washington, DC: Government Printing Office.

———. 1998. "Money Income in the U.S.: 1997." In *Current Population Reports, Consumer Income.* PP. 60-200. Washington, DC: Government Printing Office.

———. 1998. *Measuring 50 years of Economic Change.* Washington, DC: Government Printing Office.

van den Berg, L., R. Drewett, L. H. Klaassen, A. Rossi, and C. H. T. Vijverberg. 1982. *Urban Europe: A Study of Growth and Decline.* Oxford, UK: Pergamon.

Veltz, Pierre. 1996. *Mondialisation villes et territoires.* Paris: Presses Universitaires De France.

Vidal, Sarah, Jean Viard, et al. 1990. *Le deuxième sud, Marseille ou le present incertain.* Arles: Editions Actes Sud, Cahiers Pierre-Baptiste.

Vieillard-Baron, Herve. 1991. "Le risque du ghetto." *Esprit* (February):14-22.

Von Petz, U. and K. Schmals, eds. 1992. *Metropole, Weltstadt, Global City: Neue Formen der Urbanisierung.* Dortmund: Dortmunder Beiträge zur Raumplanung Vol. 60. Dortmund, Germany: Universität Dortmund.

Waldinger, Roger. 1996. *Still the Promised City? African-Americans and the New Immigrants in Postindustrial New York.* Cambridge, MA: Harvard University Press.

Walter, I. 1989. *Secret Money.* London: Unwin Hyman.

Walters, Pamela Barnhouse. 1985. "Systems of Cities and Urban Primacy: Problems of Definition and Measurement." In *Urbanization in the World-Economy,* edited by M. Timberlake. Orlando, FL: Academic Press.

Walton, John and David Seddon. 1994. *Free Markets & Food Riots: The Politics of Global Adjustment.* Cambridge, MA: Blackwell.

Ward, K., ed. 1990. *Women Workers and Global Restructuring.* Ithaca, NY: ILR Press.

Wentz, Martin, ed. 1991. *Stadtplanung in Frankfurt: Wohnen, Arbeiten, Verkehr.* Frankfurt and New York: Campus.

Werth, M. and H. Korner, eds. 1991. *Immigration of Citizens from Third Countries into the Southern Member States of the European Community. Social Europe.* Supplement 1/91. Luxembourg: Office for Official Publications of the European Communities.

Whiteman, J., J. Kipnis, and R. Burdett. 1992. *Strategies in Architectural Thinking.* Chicago/Cambridge, MA: Chicago Institute for Architecture and Urbanism/MIT Press.

WIACT (Workers' Information and Action Centre of Toronto). 1993. "Trends in Employee Home Employment." Toronto: WIACT (Mimeo).

Wigley, M. 1992. "Untitled: The Housing of Gender." Pp. 327-90 in *Sexuality and Space,* edited by Beatriz Colomina. Princeton Papers on Architecture. Princeton, NJ: Princeton Architectural Press.

Wihtol de Wenden, Catherine, ed. 1988. *La citoyenneté.* Paris: Edilic, Fondation Diderot.

Willoughby, K. W. 1990. *Technology Choice.* Boulder and San Francisco: Westview.

Wilpert, Czarina. 1998. "Migration and Informal Work in the New Berlin: New Forms of Work or New Sources of Labor?" *Journal of Ethnic and Migration Studies* 24(2):269-94.

Wilson, W. J. 1987. *The Truly Disadvantaged: The Inner City, the Underclass and Public Policy.* Chicago: University of Chicago Press.

World Bank. 1991. *Urban Policy and Economic Development: An Agenda for the 1990s.* Washington, DC: World Bank.

———. 1998. *World Development Indicators.* Washington, DC: World Bank.

"World Business." 1989. *Wall Street Journal.* September 22.

"World Business." 1992. *Wall Street Journal.* September 24, R27.

"World Business." 1998. *Wall Street Journal.* September 28, R25-27.

Wright, Talmadge. 1997. *Out of Place.* Albany: State University of New York Press.

Yamanaka, Keiko. 1991. "Asian and Latin American Workers in Japan: Should Japan Open the Unskilled Labor Market?" Department of Sociology, Grinnell College, Grinnell, IA.

Zelinksy, Wilbur. 1991. "The Twinning of the World: Sister Cities in Geographic and Historical Perspective." *Annals of the Association of American Geographers* 81(1):1-31.

Zukin, S. 1991. *Landscapes of Power.* Berkeley: University of California Press.

Glossary/Index